The Real Meat Cookbook

The Real Meat

50 CLASSIC RECIPES FOR CARNIVORES

Cookbook

consultant editor **Linda Fraser**

southwater

This edition is published by Southwater

Southwater is an imprint of
Anness Publishing Limited
Hermes House
88-89 Blackfriars Road
London
SE1 8HA
tel. 020 7401 2077
fax 020 7633 9499

Distributed in the USA by
Anness Publishing Inc.
27 West 20th Street
Suite 504
New York
NY 10011
tel. 212 807 6739
fax 212 807 6813

Distributed in the UK by
The Manning Partnership
251-253 London Road East
Batheaston
Bath BA1 7RL
tel. 01225 852 727
fax 01225 852 852

Distributed in Australia by
Sandstone Publishing
Unit 1, 360 Norton Street
Leichhardt
New South Wales 2040
tel. 02 9560 7888
fax 02 9560 7488

Southwater is an imprint of Anness Publishing Limited
© 1998, 2000 Anness Publishing Limited

1 3 5 7 9 10 8 6 4 2

Publisher: Joanna Lorenz
Senior Cookery Editor: Linda Fraser
Introduction: Jenni Fleetwood
Designer: Brian Weldon
Indexer: Hilary Bird
Photography: Karl Adamson, Edward Allwright, Steve Baxter, James Duncan, Michelle Garrett,
Amanda Heywood, William Lingwood, David Jordan, Patrick McLeavey and Tom Odulate
Food for Photography: Jacqueline Clark, Joanna Farrow, Nicola Fowler, Shirley Gill, Wendy Lee, Sue
Maggs, Lucy McKelvie, Jenny Shapter, Janet Smith and Steven Wheeler
Recipes: Catherine Atkinson, Alex Barker, Carla Capalbo, Kit Chan, Maxine Clark, Matthew Drennan,
Christine France, Sarah Gates, Shirley Gill, Soheila Kimberley, Lesley Mackley, Norma MacMillan,
Jenny Stacey, Hilaire Walden, Steven Wheeler and Jeni Wright

Notes
For all recipes, quantities are given in both metric and imperial measures and, where appropriate,
measures are also given in standard cups and spoons. Follow one set, but not a mixture, because they are
not interchangeable.

Standard spoon and cup measures are level.
1 tsp = 5 ml, 1 tbsp = 15 ml, 1 cup = 250 ml/8 fl oz

Australian standard tablespoons are 20 ml. Australian readers should use 3 tsp in place of 1 tbsp for
measuring small quantities of gelatine, cornflour, salt, etc.

Size 3 (medium) eggs are used unless otherwise stated.

Regulations relating to beef and beef products vary in different countries. If you prefer, use chicken,
lamb or vegetable stock in place of home-made beef stock.

Previously published as *Step-by-step 50 Classic Meat Dishes*

CONTENTS

INTRODUCTION

Packed with high-quality protein, meat is an excellent food. Careful rearing means leaner animals and hence healthier cuts, making it perfectly possible to follow current dietary advice while still enjoying meat and poultry.

A good butcher is the cook's best ally. Sensing this, most supermarkets have resident butchers to advise on cuts and cooking methods, and to prepare specialities like rolled and stuffed loin of pork. Local butchers often prove even more helpful, getting to know their customers' likes and dislikes.

Lean fresh meat is easy to identify – unlike processed foods or pastries, which often have hidden fat, with meat the maxim is what you see is what you get. If obvious fat has been removed and the meat looks lean, it *is* lean.

Poultry is available in a wide array of packs, from portions, such as breasts, thighs or drumsticks, to whole birds. You can buy portions on or off the bone; with or without the skin; spiced, seasoned or marinated. Whole chickens are frequently flavoured with lemon, herbs or garlic. Turkey is inexpensive and very versatile – cubes can often be substituted for red meat in casseroles, while breasts make excellent escalopes. Duck breasts are delicious.

Making meat part of a healthy diet is largely a question of balance. It is not necessary to eat vast quantities – a simple salad, satay or stir-fry will deliver plenty of flavour with the minimum of meat. Family favourites like Chilli con Carne, Irish Stew, fruity Lamb Tagine and Cassoulet may have originally evolved with economy in view, but the way they match small amounts of meat with generous quantities of vegetables, fruit, pulses or pasta makes them perfect for today's healthier lifestyle.

Meat and Poultry Cuts

Shopping for meat can be bewildering. The range of cuts is wider than ever, with a proliferation of packs offering portions of various sizes, many of them trimmed to meet the customer demand for leaner meat. Meat is marinated, spiced, supplied with sauces; available whole, sliced or diced. Recipes indicate which cut to choose, but if you are in any doubt, ask the butcher.

CHICKEN
Roast chicken makes a tasty and economical meal, especially if the carcass is used to make soup. Choose corn-fed or free-range birds for the best flavour. Cuts include breasts, legs, wings and thighs. Boneless thighs or breasts are a good buy.

DUCK
There isn't a lot of meat on a duck, so buy big rather than small birds. Although leaner than it used to be, duck is still a fatty meat, so prick birds thoroughly all over before roasting. (You may have to drain off some of the fat from the roasting tin halfway through cooking.) Breasts are excellent for quick cooking methods, such as grilling and pan-frying.

TURKEY
A turkey isn't just for Christmas – today's smaller birds are perfect for Sunday lunches, and turkey steaks are great for stir-fries or escalopes. Don't neglect diced turkey, which is good for curries and casseroles.

PHEASANT
Wild pheasant is seasonal. Find it in specialist butchers. Hen birds are generally held to be more tender than cock birds.

BEEF JOINTS
Boneless joints are sold in various weights, some with a thin layer of added fat to keep the meat moist during cooking. Sirloin, rib, rump and fillet are best for roasting (fillet is particularly good in a pastry crust); topside and silverside are better pot-roasted.

BEEF STEAKS
Rump scores highly in terms of flavour, while sirloin is generally more tender and fillet almost melts in the mouth. The best steaks come from a butcher who really knows his trade. For beef olives, ask for thin slices of topside cut across the grain.

MINCED BEEF

Wonderfully versatile. Generally speaking, the paler the mince, the higher the fat content. Lean mince (often labelled steak mince) is widely available. Read the label and be sure to observe the "use-by" date.

STEWING BEEF

The best cuts for stewing are neck (clod or sticking), blade, chuck, flank, leg and skirt.

CALF'S LIVER

Tender, economical and highly nutritious, calf's liver is also highly perishable, so use it as soon as possible after purchase.

LAMB JOINTS

Whole leg of lamb is the favourite roasting joint, although shoulder is more economical. Pot-roasting works well for leg of lamb.

MINCED LAMB

Paler than beef, minced lamb is the essential choice for classic Mediterranean dishes, such as Moussaka and Pastitsio, and for traditional dishes, such as Shepherd's Pie.

STEWING LAMB

The best cuts for stewing are middle neck, shoulder, breast, scrag end and chump chops. Trim off any excess fat before using in slow-cooked stews and casseroles.

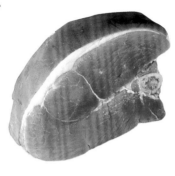

PORK/GAMMON JOINTS

For roasting, choose leg or loin. Pork cured in brine is called gammon. Baked gammon is delicious, especially with a classic Cumberland sauce.

SPARE RIBS

Cut from the belly after the main joint has been removed, these bones have small portions of very tasty meat. Usually baked, grilled or barbecued in a spicy sauce.

BACON

Used in meat cooking to add flavour or as a wrap to keep meat moist during cooking. Streaky bacon is best for this. Bacon can be bought sliced, in lardons (thin strips or dice), or in a piece. Available smoked or unsmoked (green).

SAUSAGES

The range is vast. Aside from regular pork or beef sausages, there are country-style variations that include herbs, leeks, cheese or other fillings. Pepperoni (above) is a spicy Italian sausage flavoured with red peppers. It must be cooked before being eaten.

RABBIT

This often underrated meat is low in fat and has an excellent flavour. It makes a fine pie.

Flavourings and Oils

You don't need a vast store cupboard to be a successful cook, but a few carefully selected flavourings and the right oils can make all the difference to your favourite dishes.

Anchovies

These canned fish have been filleted and salted before being packed in oil. They are traditional partners for several meat dishes, either as a garnish or in sauces, when they dissolve to enrich the flavour.

Passata

Smooth and full-flavoured, this is simply sieved puréed tomatoes. Use it as the basis of soups, casseroles, pot-roasts or pasta sauces. Sold in jars, it should be kept in the fridge after opening and used as soon as possible.

Soy Sauce

Made from fermented soya beans, soy sauce is available in dark and light varieties. Dark soy sauce has a richer flavour and is widely used in marinades, sauces and stir-fries. Use light soy sauce when only a hint of soy flavour is required. Soy sauce is salty, so check before adding extra salt.

Sun-dried Tomato Paste

Sun-dried tomato paste is richer and has a fuller flavour than regular tomato paste or purée.

Sun-dried Tomatoes

A popular ingredient, sun-dried tomatoes have a concentrated flavour that really peps up stews and minced meat mixtures. Sun-dried tomatoes preserved in oil are ready to use; dried tomatoes must be soaked in water first.

Extra Virgin Olive Oil

First pressing olive oil is a lovely, rich, green colour and has a wonderful taste. It is superb in salads and on pasta, but the flavour can be somewhat overwhelming; for frying, use a light olive oil or mix it with sunflower oil. Olive oils are like wines – they vary enormously from producer to producer and year to year. If you find one that really suits your palate, stick with it.

Above, from left: sesame oil, sun-dried tomatoes in oil, canned anchovies in oil and light soy sauce.

Left, from left: passata, extra virgin olive oil, sun-dried tomato paste and sunflower oil.

Sesame Oil

A few drops of this flavoursome oil, added to stir-fries, marinades, dressings, noodles or pasta just before serving, really boosts the taste. Don't use it for frying, as it burns at a low temperature.

Sunflower Oil

This light oil has no flavour of its own and is ideal for frying. It can be mixed with more highly flavoured oils, such as extra virgin olive oil.

Herbs and Spices

The judicious use of herbs and spices makes all the difference to meat cookery.

Bouquet Garni

A popular flavouring for stews and casseroles, a bouquet garni classically consists of a bay leaf and a sprig each of parsley and thyme, bound with kitchen string. A length of leek or celery is sometimes added. Tie the end of the string to the pan handle for easy removal. A bouquet garni sachet filled with chopped, mixed dried herbs is a convenient, though less flavourful, substitute for the real thing.

Caraway Seeds

Small brown seeds with a warm, pungent, aniseed flavouring. They combine well with pork as well as potatoes, cabbage, onions and cheese. Used in both sweet and savoury dishes.

Chillies, Chilli Powder and Crushed Chillies

There are scores of varieties of fresh chilli, ranging from mild to fiery, and shaped like miniature peppers or pods. To reduce the heat, remove the seeds before cooking. Chilli powders come in various strengths, some with added herbs and spices. Crushed chillies are widely used in Indian dishes.

Dill Weed

Fresh dill is light and feathery. It looks pretty on the plate and imparts a delicate aniseed flavour. It is widely used in Scandinavian cooking.

Fresh Coriander, Coriander Seeds and Ground Coriander

Leaf coriander is easy to grow and has a wonderful aroma. The taste is mild but distinctive – spicy and earthy. Sprinkle it over a dish at the end of cooking or use it as a garnish. Coriander seeds taste quite different. Dry roasted and freshly ground, they have a heady aroma with a burnt orange taste. Ground coriander is used in curries and tagines.

Ground Cumin and Cumin Seeds

Often used with ground coriander, cumin is another popular curry spice that also goes well with cheese, fish and vegetables. It has a strong, slightly bitter taste.

Ground Ginger/Fresh Root Ginger

Ground ginger is not widely used in meat cookery, but finds its way into some curry powders. Fresh root ginger is a favourite Chinese ingredient, used as an aromatic in stir-fries and similar dishes. It is particularly good with chicken. Buy plump, smooth roots and store them, tightly wrapped, in the fridge for a few weeks, or in the freezer. Frozen ginger grates easily and thaws on contact with hot food.

Juniper Berries

The familiar flavouring in gin, juniper berries are used in meat cookery to add a rich, gamey taste. Crushing them releases their flavour fully.

Kaffir Lime Leaves

These aromatic leaves are dark green, shiny and joined in pairs. They are widely used in Indian, Indonesian and Thai dishes. Add them whole and remove them before serving, or chop them and incorporate them in the dish. Kaffir lime leaves can be difficult to track down; if you find a supply, buy plenty and store them in the freezer, wrapped in polythene.

Above, clockwise from top left: bouquet garni, chillies (fresh, crushed, powder), juniper berries, kaffir lime leaves, turmeric, oregano (fresh, dried), fresh dill, coriander (fresh, seeds, ground), caraway seeds; *centre*: cumin (ground, seeds), ginger (ground, fresh).

Oregano

Synonymous with Italian and Greek cooking, this herb has a distinctive, pungent flavour.

Turmeric

An aromatic ground spice that imparts a brilliant yellow colour to food. It is used to colour rice or curried dishes and is one of the ingredients in curry powder.

Equipment

Sharp knives and good pans are probably top of the list of desirable items when it comes to cooking meat, but there are several other pieces of equipment that will make your task easier.

Casseroles

Flameproof casseroles are the best choice for making meat stews and pot-roasts as they can be used on the hob for browning meat or vegetables before being transferred to the oven for slow cooking.

Chopping Boards

Have at least two rigid nylon boards, reserving one for cutting raw meat and poultry. Wash them thoroughly after every use.

Colanders

Metal colanders are invaluable for draining large quantities of food, like potatoes, pasta or rice. Draining browned mince or meat cubes in a colander gets rid of excess fat and makes for healthier casseroles, stews, sauces and bakes.

Cutters

Metal cutters make short work of cutting out pastry or bread circles for pies or for croûtes.

Grater

A good-quality, free-standing box grater with serrations of different sizes is essential, not only for cheese and vegetables, but also for grating ginger. You can even use a grater to make breadcrumbs, if you don't have a food processor.

Knives

Good knives are a cook's best friend. It pays to buy the highest quality you can afford. For starters, invest in a cook's knife with a heavy, wide blade about 18 cm/7 in long. This is ideal for cutting meat. Paring knives – small knives with short, sharp blades, are ideal for vegetables. Buy several. There's nothing worse than having to turn down offers of help in the kitchen because you only have one decent knife!

Loaf Tin

For making meatloaf and terrines, a good quality loaf tin is needed. Line the base with non-stick baking paper before adding the mixture or use a tin with collapsible sides.

Measuring Jugs and Spoons

Use graduated measures for stocks and sauces, and proper measuring spoons rather than inaccurate kitchen cutlery.

Mincer

If you mince your own meat, you control how lean it is. Nothing beats an old-fashioned kitchen mincer with a selection of blades for varying the texture. A food processor can be used at a pinch, but the meat will be finely chopped, not minced.

Mixing Bowls

Buy several sizes, including a large bowl for making pastry.

Mixing Spoons

Rigid plastic spoons are preferred, as they do not absorb flavours from the food.

Pastry Brush

A small but very useful utensil, this can be used to oil roasting tins, baking dishes or pans, glaze pastry with milk or beaten egg or brush the last traces of cheese or lemon rind from a grater.

Patty Tins

Useful for making individual Yorkshire puddings or popovers.

Above, from top left: colander, sieves, mixing bowls, casserole, thermometer, grater; *on the patty tins*: knives, pastry brush, mixing spoon; *on the chopping board*: cutters, mincer, garlic press and salt and pepper mills.

Pots and Pans

It pays to buy good quality pans, even if you start with a cheaper set and replace them one at a time. If you like slow-cooked stews, make sure you have a pan of suitable size, with a thick, solid base that will allow you to simmer the food without scorching it. Read the labels on any pans you buy – some new pans hold the heat so well that it is vital to turn the heat down once their contents come to the

boil. Other pans may need seasoning before use.

A wok is invaluable for stir-frying and steaming. Choose a flat-bottomed wok if you are cooking on electricity, or the pan will wobble dangerously on the plate and will not heat up correctly.

You will need at least two frying pans, including a small one and a larger, deep, frying pan that comes with a lid.

Pestle and Mortar

For grinding spices, this is the perfect tool. Dry roast the spices first, for optimum flavour. Choose a small pestle and mortar for grinding small amounts of dry spices, and a larger version for pounding such "wet" ingredients as fresh ginger.

Roasting Tins

Rather than buy two roasting tins of the same size, choose one that will amply accommodate the Sunday joint, and a smaller tin for items like roasted vegetables or for Yorkshire pudding. Check that the tins are absolutely level. If you are replacing an existing roasting tin, do not throw the old tin away. Save it for the barbecue.

Slotted Spoon

One of the most useful kitchen utensils, this enables you to fish whole spices out of stews, transfer browned meat cubes from frying pan to casserole and drain deep fried items.

Left, hanging: large saucepan, frying pans; *below from left*: roasting tins, nylon chopping board and heavy-based flameproof casserole.

Below, from left: slotted spoons, mortars and pestles and heat-proof glass measuring jugs.

Trimming and Chopping Meat

Use a sharp cook's knife for preparing meat, and use a board kept especially for the purpose.

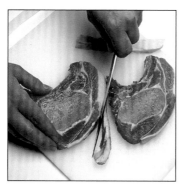

1 Preparing meat for stir-frying: Trim away any excess fat. Using a sharp knife, cut or chop the meat as required for the recipe. Keep the pieces fairly small and of uniform size, so they take the same time to cook.

2 Trimming pork chops: Use a sharp knife to cut away any rind and excess fat, leaving a little of the fat in place if the chops are to be grilled. Snip this fat several times with scissors to stop it curling during cooking.

3 Trimming lamb cutlets: Trim off excess fat with a sharp knife, then cut and scrape away all fat and gristle from the ends of the protruding bones. Cover the bone ends with foil to prevent charring.

Preparing Veal and Poultry Escalopes

Escalopes are beaten-out portions of veal or poultry that are crumbed and then shallow fried.

1 Veal escalopes: Trim any fat and gristle from around the edge of the veal escalopes (1 cm/½ in slices from the fillet end of the leg). Place the slices in turn between sheets of clear film. Using the smooth side of a meat mallet or the roller of a rolling pin, pound the meat gently but firmly all over to flatten it to a thickness of about 3 mm/ ⅛ in. It will very nearly double in size.

2 Poultry escalopes: Chicken or turkey breast fillets can be treated in exactly the same way. If the breasts are very thick, slice them horizontally in half before pounding them.

Preparing Meat for Roasting

Joints are sold ready for the oven, but you may want to give the meat a special treatment to boost the flavour.

1 Tying a boned joint: If you stuff a boned joint yourself, it will need to be rolled and tied before roasting. Reshape the meat neatly, make sure any stuffing is evenly distributed, then bind with butcher's string at 2.5 cm/1 in intervals.

2 Preparing a leg of lamb for roasting: Rub the joint with oil or butter and season with pepper. For extra flavour, make tiny slits in the surface of the joint and insert a sliver of garlic and a fresh rosemary leaf in each. Alternatively, use slices of fresh root ginger with lime rind.

3 Insert a meat thermometer through the thickest part of the joint, without touching the bone. Roast for the recommended time; for pink lamb, the temperature should be 57°C/135°F; for well done meat, it should reach 71°C/160°F. •

Stuffing and Trussing a Chicken

Trussing a chicken, especially if it is stuffed, maintains a good shape, and makes sure the stuffing doesn't escape.

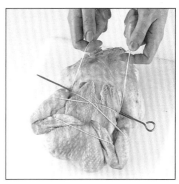

1 Stuff the small neck end of the bird, not the large cavity, as the heat from the oven may not penetrate this area. Do not pack the stuffing too tightly. Fold the neck flap neatly under the chicken and tuck the wing tips under to hold the flap in place.

2 With the chicken on its back, press the legs down to improve the shape. Push a skewer through the bird, below the thigh bone, then turn it over. Loop string round the wings, crossing it over, then take the string under the ends of the skewer.

3 Criss-cross the string over the back of the chicken, then, still holding the ends of the string, carefully turn the bird over on to its back. Bring the string up to tie the drumsticks and the parson's nose together neatly.

Jointing a Chicken

For casseroles, it is often more economical to buy a whole chicken and joint it yourself, rather than buy chicken portions.

Mincing Meat

A wide range of minced meats is available, but for special mixtures it is often desirable to mince your own.

1 Holding the chicken firmly, cut the skin between the leg and breast. Press the leg down to expose the ball-and-socket joint, cut or break the joint apart and cut down towards the parson's nose to release the leg joint. Repeat on the other side.

2 Feel for the end of the breastbone, and cut diagonally through to the ribcage. Use a pair of poultry shears or strong kitchen scissors to cut through the ribcage and wishbone, separating the two wing joints.

1 A mincer produces the most uniform minced meat, and you can vary the texture, depending on which blade is used. Trim the meat well, cut it into 4 cm/1½ in cubes or strips, then feed it through the machine.

2 A food processor will produce a somewhat different result, chopping rather than grinding the meat. Trim the meat and remove all gristle, then cut it into cubes. Fit a metal blade in the processor, add the meat and chop, using the pulsing action.

3 With clean hands, gently twist the wing tip (pinion) and tuck it under the breast meat on each wing joint in turn so that the joint is held flat. This gives it a good shape for cooking. Cut the leg joints in half if you like.

4 Use the shears to cut the breast meat from the carcass in one piece, so that all that remains is half the ribcage and the backbone, with the parson's nose attached. Cut the breast in two pieces, though the breastbone, if you like.

3 When the machine is switched off between pulses, stir the meat around so that it will be chopped evenly. Take care not to process the meat to a purée, particularly if making hamburgers, or they will be tough.

4 If you have neither mincer nor food processor, cubed meat can be minced by hand. Use a large chef's knife. Holding the tip of the blade down, raise and lower the knife by the handle, changing the position often, until the meat is fairly finely chopped.

Marinating Meat

Marinating is the soaking of food such as poultry or meat in a moist mixture prior to cooking, and is usually done to ensure that the food does not dry out when grilled or barbecued. As a bonus, marinades tenderize and add flavour.

1 Place the food for marinating in a shallow bowl or dish, large enough to hold all the pieces in a single layer. If marinating a joint, use a dish that will hold it fairly snugly.

2 Mix the marinade. An oil-based marinade is used for dry meats such as poultry; a wine or vinegar-based marinade is used for rich meats with a higher fat content.

3 Pour the marinade over the food, then turn the portions with tongs to coat them evenly. If there are herbs in the marinade, make sure they are evenly distributed.

4 Cover the dish and set it aside. If marinating for more than 30 minutes, put the dish in the fridge. Turn the portions occasionally, spooning the marinade over.

5 Lift out the marinated food, drain it and reserve or discard the marinade, according to the recipe. If necessary, let the food come to room temperature before cooking.

6 The marinade can be used for basting or brushing food during cooking, but take care if using an oil-based marinade on barbecued food, as it could cause flare-ups.

QUICK MARINADES

For meat, mix 45 ml/3 tbsp each of sunflower oil and dry sherry with 15ml/1 tbsp each of Worcestershire sauce and dark soy sauce. Add crushed garlic and pepper.

For poultry, mix 120 ml/ 4 fl oz/½ cup dry white wine with 60 ml/4 tbsp olive oil, 15 ml/1 tbsp lemon juice and 30 ml/2 tbsp chopped fresh herbs. Add pepper to taste.

Browning Meat Cubes for Stewing

Starting a stew by searing the meat ensures that the flavour is sealed in; long, slow cooking produces a tender result.

1 Trim the meat and cut it into cubes or strips, as required for the recipe. Pat dry with kitchen paper. If the meat needs to be coated in seasoned flour, do this in a strong plastic bag.

2 Heat a little oil in a frying pan or flameproof casserole until very hot. Fry a few cubes at a time until browned on all sides. As each cube browns, lift it out of the pan.

3 Cook any vegetables required in the fat remaining in the pan, then drain off the excess oil. Return the browned meat cubes to the pan and mix well.

4 Pour over liquid to cover and stir to mix. Add any herbs or flavourings and bring the liquid to the boil. Lower the heat, cover and simmer the stew for the time suggested in the recipe.

Dry frying Mince

Dry frying is an excellent way of sealing mince at the start of cooking, since it is using the meat's own fat and does not require any oil.

1 Heat a non-stick frying pan gently over a low flame.

2 Add the minced meat, spreading it out with a plastic spoon to cover the base of the pan.

3 Sauté the meat for about 5 minutes or until it is evenly browned all over. If there is any excess fat, pour it off.

Pan-frying Steaks

Tender cuts of meat, such as sirloin, rump or fillet steak, are ideal for pan-frying. Use the meat juices as the basis for a sauce.

1 Trim the steaks, leaving a little fat around the edge, if you like, and pat the steaks dry with kitchen paper. If using a coating, such as crushed peppercorns, press this evenly on both sides of the meat.

2 Heat the fat (a mixture of butter and oil works well) in a frying pan. When it is hot, add the steaks in a single layer, taking care not to crowd the pan.

3 Sear the steaks quickly on both sides, then, lower the heat fractionally and cook the steaks on both sides until done to your taste. For a rare steak, allow 2–3 minutes a side.

Stir-frying

Meat for stir-frying should be cut in small cubes or strips of uniform size. In view of the short cooking time, a tender cut must be used.

1 Heat a wok or large, deep, frying pan over a moderately high heat. When the wok or pan is hot, dribble a bracelet of oil around the inner rim, so that it coats the sides.

2 Flavour the oil with aromatics, such as garlic, ginger or sesame seeds, if you like. Add the beef pieces, in batches if necessary. Cook them quickly, using a spatula to turn them over.

3 Add ingredients like mangetouts, which need less cooking time, towards the end. Toss them with the meat until they are crisp-tender. Add any sauce as specified in individual recipes.

Casseroling Chicken

One-pot meals are easy and convenient, and the long, slow cooking means that the flavours blend beautifully as the meat cooks to perfection.

1 Heat olive oil in a flameproof casserole. When it is hot, add the chicken portions, in batches if necessary. Fry, turning several times, until browned all over. Add stock, wine or a mixture of both to a depth of about 2.5 cm/1 in.

2 Tuck in a bouquet garni, or add chopped herbs, season and bring to the boil. Lower the heat, cover and cook on the hob or in a preheated 180°C/350°F/ Gas 4 oven for 1½ hours until tender.

3 Add a selection of lightly fried vegetables about halfway through cooking. Glazed button onions, mushrooms, carrots and small new potatoes would make a good mixture.

Pot-roasting

Prime cuts can be pot-roasted, but this method really comes into its own for those flavoursome joints that benefit from being seared, then cooked slowly in stock.

1 If necessary, tie the meat into a good shape. Pat it dry with kitchen paper. Heat a little oil in a flameproof casserole. When it is very hot, add the meat (or poultry) and fry until well browned all over, turning it with two spatulas.

2 Add a small amount of stock – or a mixture of stock and wine. Heat, stirring in any browned bits that have accumulated on the bottom of the pot.

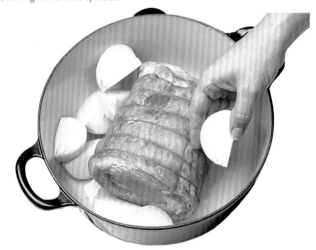

3 Arrange the vegetables around the meat. Add the remaining liquid, with seasonings or herbs. Bring to the boil, cover and simmer for 2½–3 hours, until the meat is tender. Lift out the meat and vegetables, skim the cooking juices and boil hard to make gravy.

Roasting a Chicken

Chickens have very little fat. The breast can dry out if not protected during roasting. A little butter not only keeps the bird moist, but also helps to crisp the skin.

Carving Chicken and Lamb

Poultry and meat joints should be left to stand under tented foil for 10–15 minutes after roasting before being carved to allow the juices to "settle", and make carving easier.

1 Preheat the oven to 190°C/375°F/ Gas 5. Rinse the chicken inside and out, then pat it dry. Season the cavity, then stuff the neck end, if you like. Spread the breast lightly with butter; place the bird on a rack over a roasting tin.

2 Roast the chicken for 20 minutes per 450 g/1 lb, plus 20 minutes. After the first 30 minutes, baste the bird every 10–15 minutes with the juices in the tin. If the breast starts to brown too quickly, cover it with foil.

1 Carving chicken: Holding the bird firmly with a carving fork, use a carving knife to cut between the leg and breast. Press the leg down to expose the joint, then cut through. Slip the knife under the back to remove the "oyster" with the leg.

2 With the knife at the top end of the breastbone, cut down parallel on one side of the wishbone to take a good slice of breast meat with the wing joint. As you remove the joints, arrange them neatly on a heated serving platter.

3 To test that the chicken is cooked, pierce the thickest part of the thigh with the point of a sharp knife. The juices that run out should be clear. If there is any trace of pink, roast the chicken for 10 minutes more and test again. Transfer the cooked chicken to a carving board and rest under tented foil for 10–15 minutes before carving.

3 Place the knife at the end of the breastbone and carefully cut down the front of the carcass to remove the wishbone. Hold the knife at a slight angle and cut the remaining breast meat into neat slices.

4 Carving a leg of lamb: With the thicker area uppermost, cut a wedge-shaped slice from the wider edge. This makes subsequent slicing easier. Continue to slice the meat at a slight angle down towards the bone, against the grain, then carve the other side.

Chicken and Leek Soup

A chunky chicken and vegetable soup served with garlic-flavoured fried croûtons – a meal in itself.

Serves 4

INGREDIENTS
4 boned and skinned chicken thighs
15 g/½ oz/1 tbsp butter
2 small leeks, thinly sliced
25 g/1 oz/2 tbsp long grain rice
900 ml/1½ pints/3¾ cups
    chicken stock
15 ml/1 tbsp chopped mixed fresh
    parsley and mint
salt and freshly ground black pepper
crusty bread, to serve

FOR THE GARLIC CROÛTONS
30 ml/2 tbsp olive oil
1 garlic clove, crushed
4 slices of bread, cut into cubes

parsley *mint*
long grain rice
garlic
olive oil
bread
chicken thighs
butter
leeks

1 Cut the chicken into 1 cm/½ in cubes. Melt the butter in a saucepan, add the leeks and cook until tender. Add the long grain rice and chicken and cook for a further 2 minutes.

2 Add the stock, then cover and simmer for 15–20 minutes until tender.

COOK'S TIP
To make this soup more economical, buy chicken thighs or portions with the bones and skin still intact and prepare them yourself.

3 To make the garlic croûtons, heat the oil in a large frying pan. Add the crushed garlic clove and bread cubes and cook until golden brown, stirring all the time to prevent them burning. Drain the croûtons on kitchen paper and sprinkle with a little salt.

4 Add the parsley and mint to the soup and adjust the seasoning. Garnish with some garlic croûtons, then serve with the remaining croûtons handed round separately and some crusty bread.

Mulligatawny Soup

The English army brought back the recipe for this curried chicken and rice soup from India in the eighteenth century.

Serves 4

INGREDIENTS

50 g/2 oz/4 tbsp butter or
  60 ml/4 tbsp oil
2 large chicken joints, about
  350 g/12 oz each
1 onion, chopped
1 carrot, chopped
1 small swede, chopped
about 15 ml/1 tbsp curry powder,
  to taste
4 cloves
6 black peppercorns, lightly crushed
50 g/2 oz/¼ cup lentils
900 ml/1½ pints/3¾ cups
  chicken stock
40 g/1½ oz/¼ cup sultanas
salt and freshly ground black pepper

butter • cloves • carrot • chicken • curry powder • onion • chicken stock • black peppercorns • swede • lentils

1 Melt the butter or heat the oil in a large saucepan, then cook the chicken over a brisk heat until browned. Transfer the chicken to a plate.

2 Add the onion, carrot and swede to the saucepan and cook, stirring occasionally, until the vegetables are lightly coloured. Stir in the curry powder, cloves and black peppercorns and cook for 1–2 minutes, then add the lentils. Pour the chicken stock into the saucepan, bring to the boil, then add the sultanas and chicken and any juices from the plate. Cover and simmer gently for about 1¼ hours.

3 Remove the chicken from the pan and discard the skin and bones. Chop the flesh, return to the soup and reheat. Check the seasoning before serving the soup piping hot.

COOK'S TIP

Choose red split lentils for the best colour, although either green or brown lentils could also be used.

VARIATION

If swede is out of season or unavailable, substitute about 3 small white turnips, or use 2–3 extra carrots instead.

Rockburger Salad with Sesame Croutons

This beefy American hamburger contains a surprise layer of Roquefort cheese at the centre.

Serves 4

INGREDIENTS

900 g/2 lb lean minced beef
1 egg
1 onion, finely chopped
10 ml/2 tsp French mustard
2.5 ml/½ tsp celery salt
115 g/4 oz Roquefort or other blue cheese
1 large sesame seed loaf
45 ml/3 tbsp olive oil
1 small iceberg lettuce
50 g/2 oz rocket or watercress
120 ml/4 fl oz/½ cup French Dressing
4 ripe tomatoes, quartered
4 large spring onions, sliced
freshly ground black pepper

minced beef

rocket

olive oil

onion

egg

tomatoes

sesame seed loaf

French mustard

iceberg lettuce

spring onions

Roquefort cheese

1 Place the minced beef, egg, onion, mustard, celery salt and pepper in a mixing bowl. Combine thoroughly. Divide the mixture into 16 portions, each weighing about 50 g/2 oz.

2 Flatten the pieces between two sheets of clear film or greaseproof paper to form 13 cm/5 in rounds.

3 Place 15 g/½ oz of the cheese on eight of the thin burgers. Sandwich with the remainder and press the edges firmly. Store the burgers between pieces of clear film or greaseproof paper and chill until ready to cook.

4 To make the sesame croûtons, preheat the grill to a moderate temperature. Remove the sesame crust from the bread, then cut the crust into short fingers. Moisten with olive oil and toast evenly for 10–15 minutes.

5 Season the burgers and grill for about 10 minutes, turning once.

6 Wash the salad leaves and spin or pat dry on kitchen paper. Toss with the dressing, then distribute among four large plates. Place two burgers in the centre of each plate and arrange the tomatoes, spring onions and sesame croûtons around the edge.

Warm Duck Salad with Orange and Coriander

The rich gamey flavour of duck provides the foundation for this delicious late summer salad.

Serves 4

INGREDIENTS
1 small orange
2 boneless duck breasts
150 ml/5 fl oz/⅔ cup dry white wine
5 ml/1 tsp ground coriander seeds
2.5 ml/½ tsp ground cumin or
    fennel seeds
30 ml/2 tbsp caster sugar
juice of ½ small lime or lemon
75 g/3 oz day-old bread,
    thickly sliced
45 ml/3 tbsp olive oil
½ escarole lettuce
½ frisée lettuce
30 ml/2 tbsp sunflower or
    groundnut oil
salt and cayenne pepper
4 sprigs fresh coriander, to garnish

orange

duck breasts

lime

fresh coriander

bread

escarole lettuce

caster sugar

frisée lettuce

olive oil

sunflower oil

dry white wine

1 Halve the orange and slice thickly. Discard any stray pips and place the slices in a small saucepan. Cover with water, bring to the boil and simmer for 5 minutes to remove the bitterness. Drain and set aside.

2 Pierce the skin of the duck breasts diagonally with a small knife (this will help release the fat as they cook). Rub the skin with salt. Place a steel or cast-iron frying pan over a steady heat and cook the breasts for 20 minutes, turning once, until they are medium-rare. Transfer to a warm plate, cover and keep warm. Pour the duck fat into a small bowl and set aside for use on another occasion.

3 Heat the sediment in the pan until it begins to caramelize. Add the wine and stir to loosen the sediment. Add the coriander, cumin, sugar and orange slices. Boil quickly and reduce to a coating consistency. Sharpen with lime juice and season to taste.

4 To make the garlic croûtons, remove the crusts from the bread and discard them. Cut the bread into short fingers. Heat the olive oil in a heavy frying pan, add the bread fingers and fry until evenly brown and crisp. Season with salt, then turn out on to kitchen paper to drain.

5 Wash the salad leaves and spin or pat dry using kitchen paper. Moisten with sunflower oil and distribute among four large serving plates.

COOK'S TIP
Duck breast has the quality of red meat and is cooked either rare, medium or well done according to taste.

6 Slice the duck breasts diagonally with a carving knife. Divide the breast meat into four and lift on to each salad plate. Spoon the dressing over the top, scatter with croûtons, garnish with a sprig of coriander and serve.

Melon and Parma Ham Salad with Strawberry Salsa

Sections of cool fragrant melon wrapped with slices of air-dried ham make this a delicious salad starter.

Serves 4

INGREDIENTS
1 large melon (see Cook's Tip)
175 g/6 oz Parma or Serrano ham, thinly sliced

FOR THE SALSA
225 g/8 oz/2 cups strawberries
5 ml/1 tsp caster sugar
30 ml/2 tbsp sunflower oil
15 ml/1 tbsp orange juice
2.5 ml/½ tsp finely grated orange rind
2.5 ml/½ tsp finely grated fresh root ginger
salt and freshly ground black pepper

melon

strawberries

caster sugar

orange

sunflower oil

root ginger

Parma ham

1 Halve the melon and remove the seeds with a spoon. Cut the rind away with a paring knife, then slice the melon thickly. Chill until ready to serve.

2 To make the salsa, hull the strawberries and cut them into large pieces. Place the strawberries in a small mixing bowl with the sugar and crush them lightly to release the juices. Add the oil, orange juice, rind and ginger. Season with salt and a generous twist of black pepper.

3 Arrange the melon on a serving plate, lay the ham over the top and serve with a bowl of salsa.

COOK'S TIP
Choose a well-flavoured, ripe melon, such as cantaloupe, charentais or galia. To check that the melon is ripe, press the end opposite the stalk – if ripe, it will give to gentle pressure. Or simply smell it – a ripe melon will have a strongly perfumed aroma.

Chicken Satay

Marinate the chicken in the satay sauce overnight to allow the flavours to penetrate.

Serves 4

INGREDIENTS
4 chicken breasts
lemon slices, to garnish
lettuce leaves and spring onions,
    to serve

FOR THE SATAY SAUCE
115 g/4 oz/½ cup crunchy
    peanut butter
1 small onion, chopped
1 garlic clove, crushed
30 ml/2 tbsp chutney
60 ml/4 tbsp olive oil
5 ml/1 tsp light soy sauce
30 ml/2 tbsp lemon juice
1.5 ml/¼ tsp chilli powder or
    cayenne pepper

chicken breasts

onion

garlic

peanut
butter

chutney

lemon

olive oil

soy sauce

chilli
powder

COOK'S TIP
If you are using wooden skewers, soak them in warm water for at least 30 minutes before skewering the meat to prevent them burning.

1 Put all the satay sauce ingredients into a food processor or blender and process until smooth. Spoon into a dish.

2 Remove all bone and skin from the chicken and cut into 2.5 cm/1 in cubes. Add to the satay sauce mixture and stir to coat the chicken pieces. Cover with clear film and chill for at least 4 hours or, better still, overnight.

3 Preheat the grill or barbecue. Thread the chicken pieces on to short skewers.

4 Cook for 10 minutes, turning the skewers several times and brushing occasionally with the satay sauce. Garnish with lemon slices and serve on a bed of lettuce with spring onions.

Chicken Liver Pâté with Marsala

Although this pâté is really quick and simple to make, it has a delicious – and quite sophisticated – flavour.

Serves 4

INGREDIENTS
350 g/12 oz chicken livers,
    defrosted if frozen
225 g/8 oz/1 cup butter, softened
2 garlic cloves, crushed
15 ml/1 tbsp Marsala, brandy or
    medium-dry sherry
5 ml/1 tsp chopped fresh sage
salt and freshly ground black pepper
8 sage leaves, to garnish
Melba toast, to serve

butter

garlic cloves

sage

Marsala

chicken livers

COOK'S TIP
To make Melba toast, cook medium-sliced bread until golden brown, then cut off the crusts and carefully cut each slice in two by slipping a large sharp knife between the toasted sides. Toast, cut-side up, under a low heat until the toast curls slightly and crisps.

1 Pick over the chicken livers, then rinse and dry with kitchen paper. Melt 25 g/1 oz/2 tbsp of the butter in a frying pan, and fry the chicken livers with the crushed garlic over a medium heat for about 5 minutes, or until they are firm but still pink in the middle.

2 Transfer the livers to a blender or food processor and add the Marsala and chopped sage.

3 Melt 150 g/5 oz/10 tbsp of the remaining butter in the frying pan, stirring to loosen any sediment, then pour into the blender or processor and process until smooth. Season well.

4 Spoon the pâté into four individual pots and smooth the surface. Melt the remaining butter in a separate pan and pour over the pâtés. Chill until set. Garnish with sage leaves and serve with triangles of Melba toast.

Chicken, Bacon and Walnut Terrine

The pungent spices and wine complement the meaty flavours of this rich terrine.

Serves 8 –10

INGREDIENTS
2 boneless chicken breasts
1 large garlic clove, crushed
½ slice of bread
1 egg
350 g/12 oz bacon chops (the fattier the better), minced or finely chopped
225 g/8 oz chicken or turkey livers, finely chopped
25 g/1 oz/¼ cup chopped walnuts, toasted
30 ml/2 tbsp sweet sherry or Madeira
2.5 ml/½ tsp ground allspice
2.5 ml/½ tsp cayenne pepper
pinch each ground nutmeg and cloves
8 long streaky bacon rashers, rinded and stretched
salt and freshly ground black pepper
chicory leaves and chives, to garnish

garlic

chicken breasts

chicken livers

bread

sherry

walnuts

egg

bacon chops

streaky bacon

1 Cut the chicken into thin strips and season lightly. Mash the garlic, bread and egg together. Work in the chopped bacon (using your hands is the best way) and then the finely chopped livers. Stir in the walnuts, sherry or Madeira, spices, and seasoning to taste.

2 Preheat the oven to 200°C/400°F/Gas 6. Line a 675 g/1½ lb loaf tin with bacon rashers and pack in half the meat mixture.

3 Lay the chicken strips on top and spread the rest of the mixture over. Cover the tin with lightly greased foil, seal and press down firmly. Place the terrine in a roasting tin half full of hot water. Bake for 1–1½ hours, or until firm to the touch.

4 Remove the terrine from the oven, place weights on the top and leave to cool completely. Drain off any excess fat or liquid while the terrine is still warm.

5 When the terrine is really cold, turn it out on to a board and cut into thick slices. Serve, garnished with a few chicory leaves and chives.

COOK'S TIP
If you wish to seal the terrine for longer storage, pour melted lard over the top while the terrine is still in its tin. Leave the lard to set and form a complete seal. Store the terrine in the fridge for up to five days.

Meatballs with Porcini and Parmesan

These meatballs may be eaten hot or cold, as a main course or with pasta or rice.

Serves 3 – 4 as a main course

INGREDIENTS

10 g/¼ oz/2 tbsp dried
   porcini mushrooms
450 g/1 lb lean minced beef
2 garlic cloves, finely chopped
60 ml/4 tbsp chopped fresh parsley
45 ml/3 tbsp chopped fresh basil
1 egg
90 ml/6 tbsp fresh breadcrumbs
30 ml/2 tbsp freshly grated
   Parmesan cheese
60 ml/4 tbsp olive oil
1 onion, very finely chopped
50 ml/2 fl oz/¼ cup dry white wine
salt and freshly ground black pepper
chopped fresh parsley and a sprig,
   to garnish

porcini mushrooms

egg

minced beef

garlic

basil

parsley

breadcrumbs

Parmesan cheese

olive oil

dry white wine

onion

1 Soak the dried porcini mushrooms in 150 ml/¼ pint/⅔ cup warm water for 15 minutes. Lift out of the water and chop finely. Strain the soaking water through kitchen paper and reserve.

2 In a mixing bowl, combine the beef with the mushrooms, garlic and herbs. Stir in the egg. Add the breadcrumbs and Parmesan, and season with salt and pepper. Form the mixture into small balls 4 cm/1½ in in diameter.

3 In a large, heavy frying pan heat the oil. Add the onion and cook over a low heat until soft. Raise the heat and add the meatballs, rolling them often to brown them evenly on all sides. After about 5 minutes add the mushroom soaking water. Cook the meatballs for a further 5–8 minutes, or until they are cooked through.

4 Remove the meatballs to a warmed serving plate with a slotted spoon or spatula. Add the wine to the pan, and cook for 1–2 minutes, stirring to scrape up any residues on the bottom of the pan. Pour the sauce over the meatballs. Sprinkle with fresh parsley, and serve the dish immediately with a sprig of parsley on the side.

Beef Olives

With beef slices rolled around a mushroom and bacon filling, beef olives really do resemble their vegetable namesake.

Serves 4

INGREDIENTS

25 g/1 oz/2 tbsp butter
2 bacon rashers, finely chopped
115 g/4 oz mushrooms, chopped
15 ml/1 tbsp chopped fresh parsley
grated rind and juice of 1 lemon
115 g/4 oz/2 cups fresh
    breadcrumbs
675 g/1½ lb topside of beef, cut into
    8 thin slices
45 ml/3 tbsp plain flour
45 ml/3 tbsp sunflower oil
2 onions, sliced
450 ml/¾ pint/scant 2 cups well-
    flavoured beef stock
salt and freshly ground black pepper
chopped fresh parsley, to garnish
mashed potatoes and peas, to serve

bacon   *mushrooms*

parsley   *lemon*   *breadcrumbs*

plain flour   *butter*

sunflower oil   *onion*   *beef stock*

1 Preheat the oven to 160°C/325°F/ Gas 3. Heat the butter in a small pan, add the bacon and mushrooms and fry for about 3 minutes until cooked and golden brown, stirring frequently. Leave to cool, then mix them with the parsley, lemon rind and juice and breadcrumbs. Season with salt and plenty of pepper.

2 Spread an equal amount of the breadcrumb mixture evenly over each of the beef slices, leaving a narrow border clear around the edge.

COOK'S TIP

At the end of cooking, the onions can be puréed in a food processor or blender with a little of the stock, then stirred back into the casserole to make a smooth sauce, if you prefer.

3 Roll up the slices neatly, tucking in the ends. Tie the rolls securely with fine string, then dip them in flour to coat lightly. Heat the oil in a heavy shallow pan and fry the beef rolls until lightly browned. Remove the beef rolls from the pan and keep warm.

4 Add the onions to the pan and fry until browned. Stir in the remaining flour and cook until lightly browned. Pour in the stock, then bring to the boil, stirring, and simmer for 2–3 minutes. Transfer the beef rolls to a casserole, pour over the sauce, then cover and bake for 2 hours. Lift out the "olives" and remove the string. Return to the sauce and serve hot, garnished with parsley. Serve with mashed potatoes and peas.

Osso Buco

This famous Milanese dish is rich and hearty.
Serve with risotto or plain boiled rice.

Serves 4

COOK'S TIP
Osso buco is available from large supermarkets and good butchers. Choose pieces about 2 cm/¾ in thick.

INGREDIENTS
30 ml/2 tbsp plain flour
4 pieces of osso buco (veal shanks)
2 small onions
30 ml/2 tbsp olive oil
1 large celery stick, finely chopped
1 carrot, finely chopped
2 garlic cloves, finely chopped
400 g/14 oz can chopped tomatoes
300 ml/½ pint/1¼ cups dry
    white wine
300 ml/½ pint/1¼ cups chicken or
    veal stock
1 strip of thinly pared lemon rind
2 bay leaves, plus extra to garnish
salt and freshly ground black pepper

FOR THE GREMOLATA
30 ml/2 tbsp finely chopped fresh
    flat leaf parsley
finely grated rind of 1 lemon
1 garlic clove, finely chopped

plain flour   *onions*   *olive oil*
celery
lemon   *dry white wine*   *chopped tomatoes*
chicken stock   *parsley*   *garlic*   *carrot*

1 Preheat the oven to 160°C/325°F/ Gas 3. Season the flour with salt and pepper and spread it out in a shallow dish. Add the pieces of osso buco and turn them in the flour until evenly coated. Shake off any excess flour.

2 Slice one of the onions and separate it into rings. Heat the oil in a large flameproof casserole, then add the veal, with the onion rings, and brown the veal on both sides over a medium heat. Remove the veal shanks with tongs and set aside on kitchen paper to drain.

3 Chop the remaining onion and add it to the pan with the celery, carrot and garlic. Stir the bottom of the pan to incorporate the pan juices and sediment. Cook gently, stirring frequently, for about 5 minutes until the vegetables begin to soften slightly.

4 Add the chopped tomatoes, wine, stock, lemon rind and bay leaves, then season to taste with salt and pepper. Bring to the boil, stirring. Return the veal to the pan and coat with the sauce. Cover and cook in the oven for 2 hours or until the veal feels tender when pierced with a fork.

5 To make the gremolata, mix together the chopped parsley, lemon rind and garlic. Remove the casserole from the oven and lift out and discard the strip of lemon rind and the bay leaves. Taste the sauce for seasoning. Serve the osso buco hot, sprinkled with the gremolata and garnished with extra bay leaves.

Hungarian Beef Goulash

Beef goulash is a rich, warming stew that is
flavoured with the distinctive, pungent
Hungarian spice – paprika.

Serves 4

INGREDIENTS

30 ml/2 tbsp sunflower oil
1 kg/2¼ lb braising steak, cubed
2 onions, chopped
1 garlic clove, crushed
15 ml/1 tbsp plain flour
10 ml/2 tsp paprika
5 ml/1 tsp caraway seeds
400 g/14 oz can chopped tomatoes
300 ml/½ pint/1¼ cups beef stock
1 large carrot, chopped
1 red pepper, seeded and chopped
soured cream and pinch of paprika,
    to garnish

FOR THE DUMPLINGS

115 g/4 oz/1 cup self-raising flour
50 g/2 oz/½ cup shredded suet
15 ml/1 tbsp chopped fresh parsley
2.5 ml/½ tsp caraway seeds
salt and freshly ground black pepper

sunflower oil

onions

braising steak

plain flour

beef stock

paprika

garlic

carrot

chopped tomatoes

red pepper

self-raising flour

soured cream

1 Heat the oil in a large flameproof
casserole, add the meat and fry over a
high heat for 5 minutes, stirring, until
browned. Remove with a slotted spoon.

2 Add the onions and garlic and fry
gently for 5 minutes, until softened. Add
the flour, paprika and caraway seeds, stir
and cook for 2 minutes. Return the
browned meat to the casserole and stir
in the chopped tomatoes and stock.
Bring to the boil, cover and simmer
gently for about 2 hours.

3 Meanwhile, make the dumplings. Sift
the flour and seasoning into a bowl, add
the suet, parsley, caraway seeds and
about 45–60 ml/3–4 tbsp water and mix
to a soft dough. Divide into eight pieces
and roll into balls. Cover and reserve.

4 After 2 hours, stir the carrot and
pepper into the goulash and season well.
Drop the dumplings into the goulash,
cover and simmer for about 25 minutes.
Serve in individual bowls topped with a
spoonful of soured cream and sprinkled
with a pinch of paprika.

Irish Stew

Tender, slow-cooked lamb and vegetables make this a welcome dish on a cold winter's night.

Serves 4

INGREDIENTS
4 smoked streaky bacon
    rashers, chopped
2 celery sticks, chopped
2 large onions, sliced
8 middle neck lamb chops, about
    1 kg/2¼ lb total weight
1 kg/2¼ lb potatoes, sliced
300 ml/½ pint/1¼ cups beef stock
    or water
25 ml/1½ tbsp Worcestershire sauce
5 ml/1 tsp anchovy sauce
salt and freshly ground black pepper
chopped fresh parsley, to garnish

*streaky
bacon*

celery

onions

beef stock

lamb chops

*Worcestershire
sauce*

potatoes

1 Preheat the oven to 160°C/325°F/ Gas 3. Fry the bacon for 3–5 minutes until the fat runs, then add the celery and a third of the onions and cook, stirring occasionally, until browned.

2 Layer the lamb chops, potatoes, vegetables and bacon and remaining onions in a heavy flameproof casserole, seasoning each layer and finishing with a layer of potatoes.

3 Gently stir the stock or water, Worcestershire sauce and anchovy sauce into the bacon and vegetable cooking juices in the pan and bring to the boil. Pour into the casserole, adding water if necessary so the liquid comes half way up the casserole.

4 Cover the casserole tightly, then transfer the casserole to the oven and cook for 3 hours, or until the meat and vegetables are tender. Serve hot, sprinkled with chopped parsley.

COOK'S TIP

The mutton that originally gave the flavour to Irish stew is often difficult to obtain nowadays, so lamb is used instead and other flavourings are added to compensate for it.

Moussaka

A popular classic, this moussaka is mildly spiced
and encased in a golden baked crust.

Serves 6

INGREDIENTS

1 kg/2¼ lb aubergines
120 ml/4 fl oz/½ cup olive oil
2 large tomatoes
2 large onions, sliced
450 g/1 lb minced lamb
1.5 ml/¼ tsp ground cinnamon
1.5 ml/¼ tsp ground allspice
30 ml/2 tbsp tomato purée
45 ml/3 tbsp chopped fresh parsley
120 ml/4 fl oz/½ cup dry white wine
salt and freshly ground black pepper

FOR THE SAUCE

50 g/2 oz/4 tbsp butter
50 g/2 oz/½ cup plain flour
600 ml/1 pint/2½ cups milk
1.5 ml/¼ tsp grated nutmeg
25 g/1 oz/⅓ cup grated
    Parmesan cheese
45 ml/3 tbsp toasted breadcrumbs

olive
oil

parsley

aubergines

tomato
purée

minced
lamb

milk

butter

plain
flour

Parmesan
cheese

onions

dry
white
wine

tomatoes

1 Cut the aubergines into 5 mm/¼ in
thick slices. Layer the slices in a colander,
sprinkling each layer with plenty of salt.
Leave to stand for 30 minutes.

2 Rinse the aubergines in several changes of cold water. Squeeze them gently with
your fingers to remove any excess water, then pat them dry on kitchen paper. Heat
some of the oil in a large frying pan. Fry the aubergine slices in batches until golden on
both sides, adding more oil when necessary. Leave the fried aubergine slices to drain
on kitchen paper while you cook the rest.

3 Plunge the tomatoes into boiling
water for about 30 seconds, then refresh
in cold water. Peel away the skins and
chop the tomatoes roughly.

4 Preheat the oven to 180°C/350°F/
Gas 4. Heat 30 ml/2 tbsp oil in a large
saucepan. Add the onions and minced
lamb and fry gently for 5 minutes, stirring
and breaking up the lamb with a wooden
spoon as it cooks.

5 Add the tomatoes, cinnamon,
allspice, tomato purée, parsley, wine and
pepper and bring to the boil. Reduce the
heat, cover with a lid and simmer gently
for 15 minutes.

6 Put alternate layers of the aubergines
and meat mixture in a shallow ovenproof
dish, finishing with a layer of aubergines.

7 To make the sauce, melt the butter
in a small pan and stir in the flour. Cook,
stirring, for 1 minute. Remove from the
heat and gradually blend in the milk.
Return to the heat and cook, stirring, for
2 minutes, until thickened. Add the
nutmeg, cheese and salt and pepper.
Pour the sauce over the aubergines and
sprinkle with the breadcrumbs. Bake for
45 minutes until golden. Serve hot,
sprinkled with extra black pepper.

Lamb Tagine

Combining meat, dried fruit and spices is typical of Moroccan cooking. A "tagine" is both the name of the stew and the traditional pot it is cooked in.

Serves 4–6

INGREDIENTS
115 g/4 oz/½ cup dried apricots
30 ml/2 tbsp olive oil
1 large onion, chopped
1 kg/2¼ lb boneless shoulder of
   lamb, cubed
5 ml/1 tsp ground cumin
5 ml/1 tsp ground coriander
5 ml/1 tsp ground cinnamon
grated rind and juice of ½ orange
5 ml/1 tsp saffron strands
15 ml/1 tbsp ground almonds
about 300 ml/½ pint/1¼ cups lamb
   or chicken stock
15 ml/1 tbsp sesame seeds
salt and freshly ground black pepper
fresh parsley, to garnish
couscous, to serve

dried apricots

olive oil

lamb

onion

*ground
cumin*

*ground
cinnamon*

*ground
coriander*

oranges

lamb stock

saffron

almonds

1 Cut the apricots in half and put in a bowl with 150 ml/¼ pint/⅔ cup water. Leave to soak overnight.

2 Preheat the oven to 180°C/350°F/Gas 4. Heat the olive oil in a flameproof casserole. Add the onion and cook gently for 10 minutes until soft and golden.

3 Stir in the lamb. Add the ground cumin, coriander and cinnamon, with salt and pepper to taste. Stir to coat the lamb cubes in the spices. Cook, stirring, for 5 minutes.

COOK'S TIP
If you do not have time to soak the apricots, use the ready-to-eat variety and add extra stock to replace the soaking liquid.

4 Add the apricots and their soaking liquid. Stir in the orange rind and juice, saffron, ground almonds and enough stock to cover. Cover the casserole and cook in the oven for 1–1½ hours until the meat is tender, stirring occasionally and adding more stock, if necessary.

5 Heat a heavy-based frying pan. Add the sesame seeds and dry fry in the pan, until golden. Sprinkle the sesame seeds over the meat, garnish with parsley and serve with couscous.

Chilli Con Carne

Simple and economical, this spicy dish is one of the most popular minced beef recipes.

Serves 4

INGREDIENTS

15 ml/1 tbsp sunflower oil
225 g/8 oz/2 cups minced beef
1 onion, quartered
5 ml/1 tsp chilli powder
15 g/½ oz/2 tbsp plain flour
30 ml/2 tbsp tomato purée
150 ml/¼ pint/⅔ cup beef stock
200 g/7 oz can chopped tomatoes
200 g/7 oz can kidney
   beans, drained
1 green pepper, seeded
   and chopped
15 ml/1 tbsp Worcestershire sauce
75 g/3 oz/½ cup long grain rice
salt and freshly ground black pepper
soured cream and chopped fresh
   parsley, to garnish

sunflower
oil

minced beef

onion

tomato
purée

plain flour

kidney
beans

green
pepper

long grain
rice

chilli
powder

Worcestershire
sauce

beef stock

chopped
tomatoes

1 Heat the oil in a large pan and fry the minced beef, onion and chilli powder for 7 minutes.

2 Add the flour and tomato purée and cook for 1 minute. Stir in the stock and tomatoes and bring to the boil.

COOK'S TIP

This is a great meat dish to make for a party. You can easily just double or treble the ingredients. Cook one or two days ahead – the flavour will improve with keeping – then simply reheat thoroughly just before serving.

3 Add the kidney beans, green pepper and Worcestershire sauce and season with salt and pepper. Reduce the heat, simmer and continue to cook for about 45 minutes.

4 Meanwhile, cook the rice in boiling salted water for 10–12 minutes. Drain well. Spoon on to a serving plate. Spoon the chilli over the rice, add a spoonful of soured cream and garnish with fresh parsley.

Coq au Vin

This classic French dish combines chicken, mushrooms, onion, bacon and herbs cooked in a rich red Burgundy wine.

Serves 4

INGREDIENTS
60 ml/4 tbsp plain flour
1.5 kg/3 lb chicken, cut into 8 joints
15 ml/1 tbsp olive oil
65 g/2½ oz/5 tbsp butter
20 baby onions
75 g/3 oz piece of streaky bacon
  without rind, diced
about 20 button mushrooms
30 ml/2 tbsp brandy
75 cl bottle red Burgundy wine
1 bouquet garni
3 garlic cloves
5 ml/1 tsp soft light brown sugar
salt and freshly ground black pepper
15 ml/1 tbsp chopped fresh parsley
  and croûtons, to garnish

flour   olive oil
chicken   butter
bouquet   button   brandy
garni   mushrooms
garlic   streaky
soft light bacon
brown sugar
baby   red
onions   wine

1 Place 45 ml/3 tbsp of the flour and some seasoning in a large plastic bag and shake each chicken joint in it until lightly coated. Heat the oil and 50 g/2 oz/4 tbsp of the butter in a large flameproof casserole. Add the onions and bacon and sauté for 3–4 minutes, until the onions have browned lightly. Add the mushrooms and fry for 2 minutes. Remove the onions, bacon and mushrooms with a slotted spoon into a bowl and reserve until needed.

2 Add the chicken pieces to the hot oil and cook until browned on all sides, about 5–6 minutes. Pour in the brandy and (standing well back from the pan) carefully light it with a match, then shake the pan gently until the flames subside. Pour on the wine, add the bouquet garni, garlic, sugar and seasoning.

COOK'S TIP
If you would prefer not to tackle jointing a whole chicken, then buy 8 small ready-prepared chicken joints, such as thighs or drumsticks, or 4 larger wing or breast portions.

3 Bring to the boil, cover and simmer for 1 hour, stirring occasionally. Return the reserved onions, bacon and mushrooms to the casserole, cover and cook for a further 30 minutes.

4 Lift out the chicken, vegetables and bacon with a draining spoon and keep hot. Remove the bouquet garni and boil the liquid rapidly for 2 minutes. Cream the remaining butter and flour together and whisk in teaspoonfuls of the mixture until the liquid has thickened slightly. Pour over the chicken and serve garnished with parsley and croûtons.

Cassoulet

A traditional French dish, this recipe is full of delicious flavours and makes a warming meal.

Serves 6

INGREDIENTS
450 g/1 lb boneless duck breasts
225 g/8 oz thick-cut streaky pork or
    unsmoked streaky bacon rashers
450 g/1 lb Toulouse or
    garlic sausages
45 ml/3 tbsp olive oil
450 g/1 lb onions, chopped
2 garlic cloves, crushed
2 x 425 g/15 oz cans cannellini
    beans, rinsed and drained
225 g/8 oz carrots, roughly chopped
400 g/14 oz can chopped tomatoes
15 ml/1 tbsp tomato purée
1 bouquet garni
30 ml/2 tbsp chopped fresh thyme
475 ml/16 fl oz/2 cups chicken
    stock
115 g/4 oz/2 cups fresh
    breadcrumbs
salt and freshly ground black pepper
fresh chopped thyme, to garnish

streaky pork

Toulouse sausages

duck breasts

carrot

tomato purée

chicken stock

thyme

onions

chopped tomatoes

olive oil

breadcrumbs

bouquet garni

garlic

cannellini beans

1 Preheat the oven to 160°C/325°F/ Gas 3. Cut the duck breasts and pork or bacon rashers into large pieces. Twist the sausages and cut into short lengths.

2 Heat the oil in a large flameproof casserole. Cook the meat in batches, until well browned. Remove from the pan with a slotted spoon and drain on kitchen paper.

3 Add the onions and garlic to the pan and cook for 3–4 minutes, or until beginning to soften, stirring frequently.

4 Stir in the beans, carrots, tomatoes, tomato purée, bouquet garni, thyme and seasoning. Return the meat to the pan and mix until well combined.

5 Add enough of the stock just to cover the meat and beans. (The cassoulet shouldn't be swimming in juices; if the mixture becomes too dry add a little more stock or water.) Bring to the boil. Cover tightly and cook in the oven for 1 hour.

COOK'S TIP

Toulouse sausages are the classic ingredient for this meaty casserole, but any good-quality, well-flavoured, chunky, fresh sausages will do instead.

6 Remove the cassoulet from the oven, add a little more stock or water, if necessary, and remove the bouquet garni. Sprinkle over the breadcrumbs and return to the oven, uncovered, for a further 40 minutes, or until the meat is tender and the top crisp. Brown under the grill, if necessary, and garnish with fresh thyme.

Chicken Korma

Yogurt and cream give this sauce a rich flavour and contrast with the spicy chicken.

Serves 4

INGREDIENTS

675 g/1½ lb chicken breasts,
   skinned and boned
30 ml/2 tbsp sunflower oil
25 g/1 oz blanched almonds
2 garlic cloves, crushed
2.5 cm/1 in piece fresh root ginger,
   roughly chopped
3 green cardamom pods
1 onion, finely chopped
10 ml/2 tsp ground cumin
1.5 ml/¼ tsp salt
150 ml/¼ pint/⅔ cup natural yogurt
175 ml/6 fl oz/¾ cup single cream
toasted flaked almonds and a fresh
   coriander sprig, to garnish
boiled rice, to serve

chicken breasts *single cream*

almonds *ground cumin*

sunflower oil

fresh root ginger *cardamom pods*

natural yogurt *onion* *garlic*

1 Cut the skinned chicken breasts into 2.5 cm/1 in cubes.

2 Heat the oil in a large frying pan and cook the chicken for 8–10 minutes or until browned. Meanwhile, put the almonds, garlic and ginger in a food processor or blender with 30 ml/2 tbsp water and process to a smooth paste. When the chicken is browned, remove from the pan with a slotted spoon and set aside.

3 Add the cardamom pods and fry for 2 minutes. Add the onion and fry for a further 5 minutes.

4 Stir in the almond and garlic paste, cumin and salt and cook, stirring, for a further 5 minutes.

5 Add the yogurt, a tablespoonful at a time, and cook over a low heat, until it has all been absorbed. Return the chicken to the pan. Cover and simmer over a low heat for 5–6 minutes or until the chicken is tender. Add the cream and simmer for a further 5 minutes. Garnish with toasted flaked almonds and coriander. Serve with boiled rice.

COOK'S TIP

Any leftover fresh root ginger will keep for several weeks in the fridge. Wrap it in kitchen paper, place in an airtight box and store in the salad drawer.

Rogan Josh

In this popular dish, the lamb is traditionally marinated in natural yogurt, then cooked with spices and tomatoes.

Serves 4

INGREDIENTS

1 kg/2¼ lb lamb fillet
45 ml/3 tbsp lemon juice
250 ml/8 fl oz/1 cup natural yogurt
5 ml/1 tsp salt
2 garlic cloves, crushed
2.5 cm/1 in piece fresh root
    ginger, grated
60 ml/4 tbsp sunflower oil
2.5 ml/½ tsp cumin seeds
2 bay leaves
4 green cardamom pods
1 onion, finely chopped
10 ml/2 tsp ground coriander
10 ml/2 tsp ground cumin
5 ml/1 tsp chilli powder
400 g/14 oz can chopped tomatoes
30 ml/2 tbsp tomato purée
toasted cumin seeds and bay leaves,
    to garnish
boiled rice, to serve

fresh root ginger

sunflower oil

bay leaves

lamb fillet

ground cumin

ground coriander

chilli powder

cumin seeds

chopped tomatoes

lemon juice

natural yogurt

 cardamom pods

 garlic

 tomato purée

onion

1 Trim away any excess fat from the meat and cut into 2.5 cm/1 in cubes. Mix together the lemon juice, yogurt, salt, half the garlic and the ginger in a bowl. Add the lamb and leave to marinate in the fridge overnight.

2 Heat the oil in a large frying pan and fry the cumin seeds for 2 minutes or until they begin to splutter. Add the bay leaves and cardamom pods and fry for a further 2 minutes.

3 Add the onion and remaining garlic and fry for 5 minutes. Stir in the ground coriander, cumin and chilli powder and fry for 2 minutes.

4 Add the marinated lamb and cook for 5 minutes, stirring occasionally.

COOK'S TIP
Don't miss out the marinating process as it both tenderizes the meat and improves the flavour. If you are short of time, then marinate for only 1–2 hours.

5 Add the tomatoes, tomato purée and 150 ml/¼ pint/⅔ cup water. Bring to the boil and reduce the heat. Cover and simmer for about 1–1½ hours or until the meat is tender. Garnish with toasted cumin seeds and bay leaves.

Liver with Onions

In this classic Venetian dish, the onions cook very slowly, to produce a sweet flavour.

Serves 6

INGREDIENTS
75 g/3 oz/⅓ cup butter
45 ml/3 tbsp olive oil
675 g/1½ lb onions, very
    finely sliced
800 g/1¾ lb calf's liver, thinly sliced
salt and freshly ground black pepper
45 ml/3 tbsp finely chopped fresh
    parsley and sprigs, to garnish
grilled polenta wedges, to serve
    (optional)

olive oil   *butter*

calf's liver

onions   *parsley*

1 Heat two-thirds of the butter with the oil in a large heavy frying pan. Add the onions, and cook over a low heat until soft and tender, about 40–50 minutes, stirring often. Season with salt and pepper. Remove to a side dish.

2 Heat the remaining butter in the pan over a moderate to high heat. When it has stopped bubbling, add the liver and brown it on both sides. Cook for about 5 minutes, or until done. Remove to a warmed side dish.

COOK'S TIP
If you prefer, use thinly sliced lamb's liver in place of the more expensive calf's liver.

3 Return the onions to the pan. Raise the heat slightly, and stir the onions to mix them into the liver cooking juices.

4 When the onions are hot, turn them out on to a heated serving platter. Arrange the liver on top, and sprinkle with parsley. Serve with grilled polenta wedges, if you like.

Minced Meat Kebabs

In the Middle East, these kebabs traditionally are barbecued but, if you prefer, they can also be cooked under a hot grill.

Serves 6–8

INGREDIENTS
450 g/1 lb lean lamb
450 g/1 lb lean beef
1 large onion, grated
2 garlic cloves, crushed
15 ml/1 tbsp sumac (optional)
10 ml/2 tsp bicarbonate of soda
2–3 saffron strands, soaked in
    15 ml/1 tbsp boiling water
6–8 tomatoes, halved
15 ml/1 tbsp melted butter
salt and freshly ground black pepper
chopped fresh parsley, to garnish
boiled rice, to serve

garlic
beef
tomatoes
lamb
saffron
onion
butter

COOK'S TIP

Sumac is a favourite Lebanese spice with a slightly sour but fruity flavour. It is available from most Middle Eastern food shops, but it is not essential in this recipe.

1 Mince the lamb and beef two or three times until very finely minced, place in a large bowl and add the grated onion, garlic, sumac, if using, bicarbonate of soda, soaked saffron and salt and pepper.

2 Knead by hand for several minutes until the mixture is very glutinous. It helps to have a bowl of water nearby in which to dip your fingers to stop the meat sticking. Take a small handful of meat and roll it into a ball.

3 Shape the ball around a flat skewer, moulding it around the skewer. Repeat with three or four more balls on each skewer, pressing them tightly to prevent the meat from falling off.

4 Thread the tomatoes on to skewers and prepare a barbecue. Grill the kebabs for about 10 minutes, basting them with the melted butter and turning occasionally. Garnish with parsley and serve on a bed of rice.

Peppered Steaks with Madeira

An easy, special-occasion dish – if you want to serve the steaks for a dinner party, you'll need to start marinating the steak either in the morning or the day before.

Serves 4

INGREDIENTS
15 ml/1 tbsp mixed dried
    peppercorns (green, pink
    and black)
4 sirloin or fillet steaks, about
    175 g/6 oz each
15 ml/1 tbsp extra virgin olive oil,
    plus extra for frying
1 garlic clove, crushed
60 ml/4 tbsp Madeira
90 ml/6 tbsp fresh beef stock
150 ml/¼ pint/⅔ cup double cream
salt
salad and boiled potatoes,
    to serve

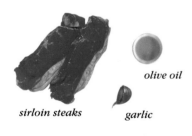

sirloin steaks *olive oil* *garlic*

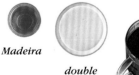

Madeira *double cream* *beef stock*

1 Finely crush the peppercorns using a pestle and mortar, then press on to both sides of the steaks.

2 Place the steaks in a shallow non-metallic dish, then add the oil, garlic and Madeira. Cover and leave to marinate in a cool place for about 4–6 hours, or preferably overnight. Remove the steaks from the dish, reserving the marinade. Brush a little oil over a heavy-based frying pan and heat until hot.

3 Add the steaks and cook over a high heat, allowing 3 minutes per side for medium or 2 minutes per side for rare. Remove and keep warm.

4 Add the reserved marinade and the stock to the pan and bring to the boil, then leave the sauce to bubble until it is well reduced. Add the cream, with salt to taste, to the pan and stir until slightly thickened. Serve the steaks with the sauce and salad and potatoes.

COOK'S TIP
Mixed green, pink and black peppercorns have an excellent flavour and add a pretty, speckled appearance to the steaks. However, if you can't find the mixed peppercorns, then use only one or two of the colours. Or simply use coarsely ground black pepper from a peppermill instead.

Beef and Mushroom Burgers

The added mushrooms and breadcrumbs give the burgers a robust flavour – and extra fibre.

Serves 4–5

INGREDIENTS
1 small onion, chopped
150 g/5 oz/2 cups small
  cup mushrooms
450 g/1 lb lean minced beef
50 g/2 oz/1 cup fresh white or
  wholemeal breadcrumbs
5 ml/1 tsp dried mixed herbs
15 ml/1 tbsp tomato purée
plain flour, for shaping
salt and freshly ground black pepper
relish and salad leaves,
  to garnish
soft burger buns or pitta bread,
  to serve

mushrooms

tomato purée

minced beef

plain flour

dried mixed herbs

onion

breadcrumbs

1 Place the onion and mushrooms in a food processor or blender and process until finely chopped. Add the minced beef, white or wholemeal breadcrumbs, dried herbs and tomato purée. Season with plenty of salt and pepper. Process for a few seconds more, until the mixture binds together but still has a little texture.

2 Divide the mixture into eight to ten pieces, then press into burger shapes using lightly floured hands.

3 Cook the burgers in a non-stick frying pan, or under a hot grill for about 12–15 minutes, turning once, until well browned and evenly cooked.

4 Lift the burgers out of the pan and place in the burger buns or pitta bread with relish and salad leaves to garnish.

COOK'S TIP

The mixture is quite soft, so handle it carefully and use a fish slice for turning to prevent the burgers from breaking up during cooking. If you have time, chill the burgers for about half an hour before cooking to allow them to firm up slightly.

Beef Strips with Orange and Ginger

A quick and easy dish made with tender strips of beef and vegetables in a tangy sauce.

Serves 4

INGREDIENTS

450 g/1 lb beef rump, fillet or
   sirloin, trimmed of fat and cut
   into thin strips
finely grated rind and juice of
   1 orange
15 ml/1 tbsp light soy sauce
5 ml/1 tsp cornflour
2.5 cm/1 in piece fresh root ginger,
   finely chopped
10 ml/2 tsp sesame oil
1 large carrot, cut into thin strips
2 spring onions, thinly sliced
rice noodles or boiled rice,
   to serve

beef

orange

soy sauce

sesame oil

cornflour

carrot

spring onions

fresh root ginger

1 Place the beef strips in a bowl and sprinkle over the orange rind and juice. If possible, leave to marinate for at least 30 minutes.

2 Drain the liquid from the meat and set aside, then mix the meat with the soy sauce, cornflour and ginger.

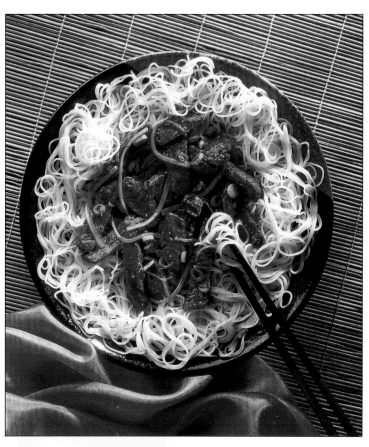

3 Heat the oil in a wok or frying pan and add the beef. Stir-fry for 1 minute until lightly coloured, then add the carrot and stir-fry for 2–3 minutes.

4 Stir in the spring onions and reserved liquid, then cook, stirring, until boiling and thickened. Serve hot with rice noodles or plain boiled rice.

VARIATION

This dish would be equally good with thin strips of lean lamb, chicken breast or turkey.

COOK'S TIP

It is important that the wok or frying pan is very hot before adding the marinated beef, otherwise, rather than frying and browning, it will tend to stew and not colour.

Chicken Chow Mein

Chow Mein is a classic Chinese noodle dish
stir-fried with meat, seafood or vegetables.

Serves 4

INGREDIENTS
350 g/12 oz Chinese egg noodles
225 g/8 oz skinless, boneless
    chicken breasts
45 ml/3 tbsp soy sauce
15 ml/1 tbsp rice wine or dry sherry
15 ml/1 tbsp dark sesame oil
60 ml/4 tbsp sunflower oil
2 garlic cloves, finely chopped
50 g/2 oz mangetouts, topped
    and tailed
115 g/4 oz/½ cup beansprouts
50 g/2 oz ham, finely shredded
4 spring onions, finely chopped
salt and freshly ground black pepper

egg noodles *chicken breasts* *ham*

soy sauce *rice wine* *sunflower oil*

mangetouts

spring onions

sesame oil

garlic

1 Cook the noodles in a saucepan of
boiling water according to the packet
instructions until tender. Drain, rinse
under cold water and drain well.

2 Slice the chicken into fine shreds about 5 cm/2 in in length. Place in a bowl and
add 10 ml/2 tsp of the soy sauce, the rice wine or sherry and sesame oil.

3 Heat half the sunflower oil in a wok
or large frying pan over a high heat.
When it starts smoking, add the chicken
mixture. Stir-fry for 2 minutes, then
transfer the chicken to a plate and keep
it hot. Wipe the wok clean and heat the
remaining oil. Stir in the garlic,
mangetouts, beansprouts and ham,
stir-fry for another minute or so and
then add the cooked noodles.

4 Continue to stir-fry until the noodles
are heated through. Add the remaining
soy sauce to taste and season with salt
and pepper. Return the chicken and any
juices to the noodle mixture, add the
chopped spring onions and give the
mixture a final stir. Serve immediately.

VARIATIONS

There are lots of different
ingredients that can be used for
this recipe. Try cooked, peeled
prawns, finely sliced beef or
pork, sliced mushrooms,
chopped baby sweetcorn or
shredded pak choi in addition
to or in place of some of the
meat and vegetables.

COOK'S TIP

If you have time, slice the
chicken ahead of time and leave
to marinate in the soy sauce
mixture for up to 2 hours
before cooking to tenderize it.

Chinese Spiced Spare Ribs

Fragrant with spices, this authentic Chinese dish makes a great starter to an informal meal.

Serves 4

INGREDIENTS
675–1 kg/1½–2¼ lb meaty pork
    spare ribs
25 ml/1½ tbsp cornflour
groundnut oil, for deep frying
coriander sprigs, to garnish

FOR THE SPICED SALT
5 ml/1 tsp Szechuan peppercorns
30 ml/2 tbsp coarse sea salt
2.5 ml/½ tsp Chinese five-spice
    powder

FOR THE MARINADE
30 ml/2 tbsp light soy sauce
5 ml/1 tsp caster sugar
15 ml/1 tbsp Chinese rice wine
    or sherry
freshly ground black pepper

sea salt

*pork
spare ribs*

soy sauce

cornflour

*rice
wine*

*groundnut
oil*

caster sugar

five-spice powder

*Szechuan
peppercorns*

1 Using a sharp, heavy cleaver, chop the spare ribs into pieces about 5 cm/ 2 in long or ask your butcher to do this, then place them in a shallow dish.

2 To make the spiced salt, heat a wok to a medium heat. Add the Szechuan peppercorns and sea salt and dry fry for about 3 minutes, stirring constantly, until the mixture colours slightly. Remove the wok from the heat and stir in the five-spice powder. Leave to cool.

3 Using a mortar and pestle or an electric coffee grinder, grind the spiced salt to a fine powder.

COOK'S TIP
Szechuan peppercorns have a lovely aromatic flavour. They are available from supermarkets and Chinese food shops, but if you can't find them, then use black peppercorns instead.

4 Sprinkle 5 ml/1 tsp of the spiced salt over the spare ribs and rub in well with your hands. Place the soy sauce, sugar, rice wine or sherry and some freshly ground black pepper in a bowl, then toss the ribs in the marinade until well coated. Cover and leave to marinate in the fridge for about 2 hours, turning the spare ribs occasionally.

5 Pour off any excess marinade from the spare ribs. Sprinkle the pieces with cornflour and mix well to coat evenly.

COOK'S TIP
Any leftover spiced salt can be kept for several months in a screw-top jar. Use to rub on the flesh of duck, chicken or pork before cooking.

6 Half-fill a wok with oil and heat to 180°C/350°F. Deep fry the spare ribs in batches for 3 minutes until pale golden. Remove and set aside. Reheat the oil to the same temperature. Return the spareribs to the oil and deep fry for a second time for 1–2 minutes until crisp and cooked. Drain on kitchen paper. Transfer the ribs to a warmed platter and sprinkle over 5–7.5 ml/1–1½ tsp of the spiced salt. Garnish with coriander sprigs and serve at once.

Chicken Kiev

Cut through the crisp-coated chicken to reveal a creamy filling with just a hint of garlic.

Serves 4

INGREDIENTS
4 large chicken breasts, boned
 and skinned
15 ml/1 tbsp lemon juice
115 g/4 oz/½ cup ricotta cheese
1 garlic clove, crushed
30 ml/2 tbsp chopped fresh parsley
1.5 ml/¼ tsp freshly grated nutmeg
30 ml/2 tbsp plain flour
pinch of cayenne pepper
1.5 ml/¼ tsp salt
115 g/4 oz/2 cups fresh
 white breadcrumbs
2 egg whites, lightly beaten
parsley sprigs, to garnish
duchesse potatoes, French beans
 and grilled tomatoes, to serve

chicken breasts

breadcrumbs

lemon juice

ricotta cheese

garlic

parsley

eggs

plain flour

1 Place the chicken breasts between two sheets of clear film and gently beat with a rolling pin until flattened. Sprinkle with the lemon juice.

2 Mix the ricotta cheese with the garlic, 15 ml/1 tbsp of the chopped parsley, and the nutmeg. Shape into four 5 cm/2 in long cylinders.

3 Put one portion of the cheese and herb mixture in the centre of each chicken breast and fold the meat over, tucking in all the edges to enclose the filling completely.

4 Secure the chicken with cocktail sticks pushed through the centre of each. Mix together the flour, cayenne pepper and salt. Dust the chicken with the seasoned flour.

5 Mix together the breadcrumbs and remaining parsley. Dip the chicken into the egg whites, then coat with the breadcrumbs. Chill for 30 minutes in the fridge, then dip into the egg white and breadcrumbs for a second time. Heat the oil in a heavy-based deep-frying pan to 365°F/185°C. Deep fry the chicken for 25–30 minutes until cooked through and golden brown.

6 Alternatively, bake the chicken in the oven. Preheat the oven to 200°C/400°F/Gas 6. Put the chicken on a non-stick baking sheet and spray with non-stick cooking spray. Bake in the preheated oven for 25 minutes or until the coating is golden brown and the chicken completely cooked. Remove the cocktail sticks and garnish with parsley. Serve with duchesse potatoes, French beans and grilled tomatoes.

Roast Chicken with Lemon and Herbs

Use a well-flavoured chicken for this classic dish – free-range or corn-fed would be ideal.

Serves 4

INGREDIENTS
1.3 kg/3 lb chicken
1 unwaxed lemon, halved
small bunch thyme sprigs
1–2 bay leaves
15 g/½ oz/1 tbsp butter, softened
60–90 ml/4–6 tbsp chicken stock
    or water
salt and freshly ground black pepper

chicken

butter

thyme

bay leaves

chicken stock

lemon

1 Preheat the oven to 200°C/400°F/ Gas 6. Season the chicken inside and out with salt and pepper. Squeeze the juice of one lemon half and then place the juice, the squeezed lemon half, the thyme and bay leaves in the chicken cavity. Tie the legs with string and rub the breast with butter.

COOK'S TIP
Be sure to save the carcasses of roast poultry for stock. Freeze them until you have several, then simmer with aromatic vegetables, herbs and water.

2 Place the chicken on a rack in a roasting tin. Squeeze over the juice of the other lemon half. Roast for 1 hour, basting two or three times, until the juices run clear when the thickest part of the thigh is pierced with a knife.

3 Pour the juices from the cavity into the roasting tin and transfer the chicken to a carving board. Cover loosely with foil and leave to stand for 10–15 minutes before carving.

4 Skim off the fat from the cooking juices. Add the stock or water and boil over a medium heat, stirring and scraping the base of the pan, until slightly reduced. Strain and serve with the roast chicken.

Roast Rabbit with Three Mustards

Each of the three different mustards in this recipe adds a distinctive flavour to the dish.

Serves 4

INGREDIENTS
15 ml/1 tbsp Dijon mustard
15 ml/1 tbsp tarragon mustard
15 ml/1 tbsp wholegrain mustard
1.5 kg/3–3½ lb rabbit portions
1 large carrot, sliced
1 onion, sliced
30 ml/2 tbsp chopped fresh
   tarragon
120 ml/4 fl oz/½ cup dry white wine
150 ml/¼ pint/⅔ cup double cream
salt and freshly ground black pepper
fresh tarragon, to garnish

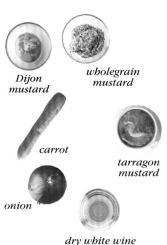

Dijon mustard *wholegrain mustard*

carrot

tarragon mustard

onion

dry white wine

 double cream   *tarragon*

rabbit portions

VARIATION
If the three different mustards are not available, use one or two varieties, increasing the quantities accordingly. The flavour will not be quite as interesting, but the dish will still taste good.

1 Preheat the oven to 200°C/400°F/ Gas 6. Mix the mustards in a bowl, then spread the mixture evenly over the rabbit portions.

2 Put the carrot and onion slices in a large roasting tin and scatter the chopped tarragon over the top. Pour in 120 ml/4 fl oz/½ cup water, then arrange the meat on top.

3 Roast for 25–30 minutes, basting frequently with the juices, until the rabbit is tender. Remove the rabbit to a heated serving dish and keep hot. Using a slotted spoon, carefully remove the carrot and onion slices from the roasting tin and discard.

4 Place the roasting tin on the hob and add the white wine. Boil to reduce by about two-thirds. Stir in the double cream and allow to bubble up for a few minutes. Season with salt and pepper and pour over the rabbit. Serve garnished with fresh tarragon.

Roast Turkey

Everyone needs a foolproof recipe for the traditional Christmas turkey, stuffing and gravy.

Serves 4

INGREDIENTS
4.5 kg/10 lb oven-ready turkey, with
   giblets (defrosted if frozen)
1 large onion, peeled, halved and
   stuck with 6 whole cloves
50 g/2 oz/4 tbsp butter, softened
10 chipolata sausages
10 bacon rolls
salt and freshly ground black pepper
mixed fresh herbs, to garnish
mixed vegetables, to serve

FOR THE STUFFING
225 g/8 oz rindless, streaky
   bacon, chopped
1 large onion, finely chopped
450 g/1 lb pork sausagemeat
25 g/1 oz/⅓ cup rolled oats
30 ml/2 tbsp chopped fresh parsley
10 ml/2 tsp mixed dried herbs
1 large egg, beaten
115 g/4 oz dried apricots,
   finely chopped

FOR THE GRAVY
25 g/1 oz/2 tbsp plain flour

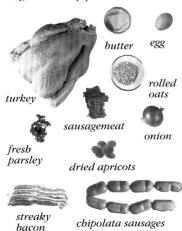

turkey   *butter*   *egg*   *rolled oats*   *onion*   *sausagemeat*   *fresh parsley*   *dried apricots*   *streaky bacon*   *chipolata sausages*

1 Preheat the oven to 200°C/400°F/ Gas 6. To make the stuffing, cook the bacon and onion gently in a pan until the bacon is crisp and the onion tender. Transfer to a large bowl and mix in all the remaining stuffing ingredients. Season with salt and pepper.

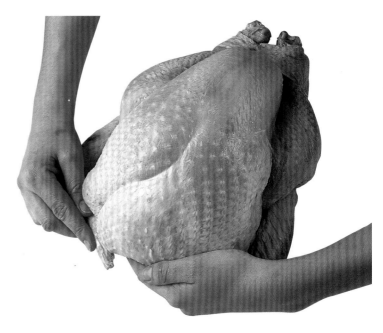

2 Stuff the neck end of the turkey only, tuck the flap of skin under and secure it with a small skewer or stitch it with thread (do not overstuff the turkey or the skin will burst during cooking). Reserve any remaining stuffing.

3 Put the onion halves studded with cloves in the body cavity of the turkey and tie the legs together. Weigh the stuffed bird and calculate the cooking time: allow 15 minutes per 450 g/1 lb plus 15 minutes over. Place the turkey in a large roasting tin.

4 Spread the turkey with butter and season with salt and pepper. Cover it loosely with foil and cook for 30 minutes. Baste the turkey with the pan juices, then lower the oven temperature to 180°C/ 350°F/Gas 4 and cook for the remainder of the calculated time (about 3½ hours for a 4.5 kg/10 lb bird). Baste it every 30 minutes or so.

5 With wet hands, shape the remaining stuffing into small balls, place in a roasting dish with the sausages and bacon rolls and set aside. Remove the foil from the turkey for the last hour of cooking and baste it. 5 minutes before the end of cooking, put the stuffing balls, sausages and bacon rolls in the oven and cook for 20 minutes, or until golden.

COOK'S TIP

Before you switch on the oven, adjust the oven shelves to allow for the size of the turkey.

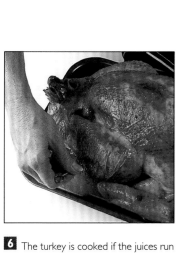

6 The turkey is cooked if the juices run clear when the thickest part of the thigh has been pierced whith a skewer. Transfer the turkey to a serving plate, cover with foil and let it stand for about 15 minutes before carving. To make the gravy, spoon off the fat from the tin, leaving the meat juices. Blend in the flour and cook for 2 minutes. Stir in the stock and bring to the boil. Check the seasoning and pour into a gravy boat. Remove the skewer or string and pour any juices into the gravy. Garnish the turkey with fresh herbs and serve it with chipolata sausages, bacon rolls, stuffing balls and mixed vegetables.

Mediterranean Chicken

This is the perfect supper-party dish – quick to prepare and full of sunshine flavours.

Serves 4

INGREDIENTS
4 chicken breast and wing portions, about 675 g/1½ lb total weight
115 g/4 oz/1 cup soft cheese with garlic and herbs
450 g/1 lb courgettes
2 red peppers, seeded
450 g/1 lb plum tomatoes
4 celery sticks
about 30 ml/2 tbsp olive oil
275 g/10 oz onions, roughly chopped
3 garlic cloves, crushed
8 sun-dried tomatoes, roughly chopped
5 ml/1 tsp dried oregano
30 ml/2 tbsp balsamic vinegar
salt and 5 ml/1 tsp paprika
olive ciabatta or crusty bread, to serve

courgettes

chicken portions

sun-dried tomatoes

red peppers

balsamic vinegar

celery

garlic cloves

onions

plum tomatoes

olive oil

dried oregano

soft cheese

1 Preheat the oven to 190°C/375°F/Gas 5. Loosen the skin of each chicken portion, without removing it, to make a pocket. Divide the cheese into four and push one-quarter underneath the skin of each chicken portion in an even layer.

2 Cut the courgettes and peppers into similarly sized chunky pieces. Quarter the tomatoes and slice the celery sticks.

3 Heat 30 ml/2 tbsp of the oil in a large, shallow flameproof casserole. Cook the onions and garlic for 4 minutes until they are soft and golden, stirring them frequently.

4 Add the courgettes, peppers and celery and cook for a further 5 minutes.

5 Stir in the tomatoes, sun-dried tomatoes, oregano and balsamic vinegar. Season well.

6 Place the chicken on top, drizzle over a little more olive oil and season with salt and paprika. Bake in the oven for 35–40 minutes or until the chicken is golden and cooked through. Serve with plenty of olive ciabatta or crusty bread.

Roast Duck with Orange

Already a popular alternative on the festive feast menu, duck and oranges make the perfect combination here.

Serves 8

INGREDIENTS
4 oranges, segmented, with rind and
    juice reserved
2 x 2.25 kg/5 lb oven-ready ducks,
    with giblets
salt and freshly ground black pepper
fresh parsley sprig, to garnish

FOR THE SAUCE
30 ml/2 tbsp plain flour
300 ml/½ pint/1¼ cups chicken or
    duck stock
150 ml/¼ pint/⅔ cup port or
    red wine
15 ml/1 tbsp redcurrant jelly

chicken stock

ducks

port

oranges

plain flour

redcurrant jelly

1 Preheat the oven to 180°C/350°F/ Gas 4. Tie the orange rind with string and place it inside the cavities of the two ducks.

2 Place the ducks on a rack in one large or two smaller roasting tins, prick the skin well, season and cook for 30 minutes per 450 g/1 lb (about 2½ hours), until the flesh is tender and the juices run clear. Carefully pour off the fat from the roasting tin(s) into a heatproof bowl halfway through the cooking time. Transfer the ducks to a carving board and remove the orange rind from the cavities.

3 To make the sauce, remove any fat from the roasting tin(s), leaving the sediment and juices behind. If using two tins, scrape the sediment and juices into one of the tins. Sprinkle in the flour and cook for 2 minutes. Blend in the rest of the ingredients and reserved orange rind, finely chopped. Bring to the boil and simmer for about 10 minutes, then strain into a pan. Add the orange segments with their juices.

4 To carve the ducks, remove the legs and wings, cutting through the joints. Cut the two end joints off the wings and discard them. Cut the breast meat off the carcass in one piece and slice it thinly. Arrange the slices on a warmed serving plate with the legs and the wing joints. Spoon over some of the hot sauce and serve the rest separately, in a sauce boat. Garnish with parsley and serve.

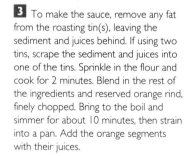

Roast Pheasant with Port

This recipe is best for very young pheasants – female birds are the most tender.

Serves 4

INGREDIENTS

2 oven-ready hen pheasants, about
675 g/1½ lb each
50 g/2 oz/4 tbsp unsalted butter,
softened
8 thyme sprigs
2 bay leaves
6 streaky bacon rashers
15 ml/1 tbsp plain flour
175 ml/6 fl oz/¾ cup game
or chicken stock, plus more
if needed
15 ml/1 tbsp redcurrant jelly
45–60 ml/3–4 tbsp port
freshly ground black pepper
fresh thyme sprigs and bay leaves,
to garnish

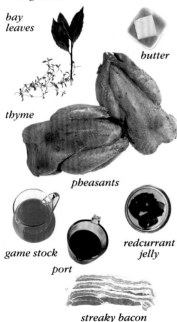

bay
leaves

butter

thyme

pheasants

game stock

port

redcurrant
jelly

streaky bacon

1 Preheat the oven to 230°C/450°F/ Gas 8. Line a roasting tin with a sheet of foil large enough to enclose the pheasants. Brush the foil with oil. Wipe the pheasants with damp kitchen paper and remove extra fat or skin. Using your fingertips, loosen the breast skin. With a round-bladed knife, spread the butter between the skin and breast meat. Tie the legs securely, then lay the thyme and bay leaf over each breast.

2 Lay bacon rashers over the breasts, place the birds in the foil-lined tin and season with pepper. Bring together the long ends of the foil, fold over securely to enclose, then seal the ends.

3 Roast the birds for 20 minutes, then reduce the oven temperature to 190°C/375°F/Gas 5 and cook for a further 40 minutes. Uncover the birds and roast for 10–15 minutes more or until they are browned and the juices run clear when the thigh of a bird is pierced with a knife. Transfer the birds to a board and leave to stand, covered with clean foil, for 10 minutes before carving.

4 Carefully pour the juices from the foil into the roasting tin and skim off any fat. Sprinkle in the flour and cook over a medium heat, stirring until smooth. Whisk in the stock and bring to the boil, stirring all the time.

5 Add the redcurrant jelly and bring to the boil. Simmer until the sauce thickens slightly, adding more stock if needed. Stir in the port and season. Strain and serve with the pheasant, garnished with herbs.

Beef Wellington with Mushrooms

Traditionally this dish calls for goose liver pâté, but mushroom pâté is cheaper and tastes equally delicious.

Serves 4

INGREDIENTS
675 g/1½ lb fillet steak, tied
15 ml/1 tbsp sunflower oil
350 g/12 oz puff pastry, defrosted
    if frozen
1 egg, beaten, to glaze
salt and freshly ground black pepper

FOR THE PARSLEY PANCAKES
50 g/2 oz/4 tbsp plain flour
150 ml/¼ pint/⅔ cup milk
1 egg
30 ml/2 tbsp chopped fresh parsley

FOR THE MUSHROOM PÂTÉ
2 shallots or 1 small onion, chopped
25 g/1 oz/2 tbsp unsalted butter
450 g/1 lb assorted wild and
    cultivated mushrooms, such as
    oyster mushrooms, ceps,
    chanterelles or closed field
    mushrooms, trimmed and
    chopped
50 g/2 oz/1 cup fresh
    white breadcrumbs, combined
    with 75 ml/5 tbsp double cream
    and 2 egg yolks

sunflower oil

puff pastry

butter

eggs

breadcrumbs

shallots

double cream

milk

plain flour

wild mushrooms

1 Preheat the oven to 220°C/425°F/ Gas 7. Season the fillet steak with several twists of black pepper. Heat the oil in a roasting tin, add the steak and quickly sear to brown all sides. Transfer to the preheated oven and roast for 15 minutes for rare, 20 minutes for medium-rare or 25 minutes for well-done meat. Set aside to cool. Reduce the temperature to 190°C/375°F/Gas 5.

2 To make the pancakes, beat the flour, a pinch of salt, half the milk, the egg and parsley together until smooth, then stir in the remaining milk. Heat a greased, non-stick pan and pour in enough batter to coat the bottom. When set, turn over and cook the other side briefly until lightly browned. Continue with remaining batter – the recipe makes three or four.

3 To make the pâté, fry the shallots in butter to soften without colouring. Add the mushrooms and cook until the juices begin to run. Increase the heat and cook briskly until the juices evaporate completely. Add the bread and cream mixture and blend to make a smooth paste. Allow to cool.

4 Roll out the pastry and cut into a 36 × 30 cm/14 × 12 in rectangle. Arrange the pancakes on the pastry and spread with pâté. Place the beef on top and spread over any remaining pâté. Cut four squares from the corners of the pastry. Moisten the edges with egg and wrap them over the meat.

COOK'S TIP

Instead of using a meat thermometer, you can insert a metal skewer into the meat. If the skewer is cold, the meat is not done, if it is warm, the meat is rare and if it is hot, it is well done.

5 Decorate the top with the reserved pastry trimmings, transfer to a baking sheet and rest in a cool place until ready to cook.

6 Brush evenly with beaten egg. Cook the Wellington for about 40 minutes until golden brown. To ensure that the meat is heated through, test with a meat thermometer. It should read 52–54°C/125–130°F for rare, 57°C/135°F for medium-rare and 71°C/160°F for well-done meat.

Baked Gammon with Cumberland Sauce

Serve this delicious cooked meat and tangy sauce either hot or cold.

Serves 8–10

INGREDIENTS

2.25 kg/5 lb smoked or unsmoked
    gammon joint
1 onion
1 carrot
1 celery stick
1 bouquet garni
6 peppercorns
whole cloves
50 g/2 oz/4 tbsp soft light brown
    or demerara sugar
30 ml/2 tbsp golden syrup
5 ml/1 tsp English mustard powder

FOR THE CUMBERLAND SAUCE
shredded rind and juice of 1 orange
30 ml/2 tbsp lemon juice
120 ml/4 fl oz/½ cup port or
    red wine
60 ml/4 tbsp redcurrant jelly

1 Soak the gammon overnight in a cool place in plenty of cold water to cover. Discard this water. Put the joint into a large pan and cover it again with more cold water. Bring the water to the boil slowly and skim off any scum from the surface with a slotted spoon.

cloves

gammon
joint

onion

port

carrot   lemon

soft light
brown sugar   celery

bouquet
garni

peppercorns

mustard
powder

golden
syrup

orange

redcurrant
jelly

COOK'S TIP

To serve the gammon cold, loosely cover the joint and leave it in a cool place until cold, then wrap more tightly in foil and transfer to the fridge until ready to carve.

2 Cut the vegetables into chunks and add to the pan with the bouquet garni and peppercorns. Cover and simmer very gently for 2 hours. (The meat can also be cooked in the oven at 180°C/350°F/Gas 4. Allow 30 minutes per 450 g/1 lb.)

3 Leave the meat to cool in the liquid for 30 minutes. Then remove it from the liquid and strip off the skin neatly with the help of a knife (use rubber gloves if the gammon is too hot to handle).

4 Score the fat in diamonds with a sharp knife and stick a clove in the centre of each diamond.

5 Preheat the oven to 180°C/350°F/ Gas 4. Put the sugar, golden syrup and mustard powder in a small pan and heat gently to melt. Place the gammon in a roasting tin and spoon over the glaze. Bake for about 20 minutes until golden brown. Put the gammon under a hot grill, if necessary, to get a good colour. Allow to stand in a warm place for 15 minutes before carving (to allow the flesh to relax and make carving easier).

6 To make the sauce, put the orange and lemon juice into a pan with the port and redcurrant jelly, and heat gently to melt the jelly. Pour boiling water on to the orange rind, drain, and add to the sauce. Cook gently for 2 minutes. Serve the sauce hot, in a sauce boat.

Pot-roast Glazed Lamb

The vegetables in this pot-roast turn tender and caramelized, full of the flavours of the meat.

Serves 6

INGREDIENTS

12 garlic cloves
1.1 kg/2½ lb leg of lamb
    (knuckle end)
about 12 small fresh rosemary sprigs
45 ml/3 tbsp olive oil
12 shallots, peeled
900 g/2 lb potatoes, cut into chunks
675 g/1½ lb parsnips, cut into
    large chunks
675 g/1½ lb carrots, cut into chunks
300 ml/½ pint/1¼ cups red wine
45 ml/3 tbsp clear honey
30 ml/2 tbsp dark soy sauce
10 ml/2 tsp plain flour
475 ml/16 fl oz/2 cups lamb stock
salt and freshly ground black pepper
fresh rosemary sprigs, to garnish

soy sauce
clear honey
rosemary
garlic
red wine
plain flour
leg of lamb
carrots
shallots
lamb stock
parsnips
potatoes
olive oil

1 Preheat the oven to 190°C/375°F/Gas 5. Peel three of the cloves of garlic and slice. Make slits all over the meat and insert slices of garlic and small sprigs of rosemary. Season well.

2 Heat the oil in a large flameproof casserole or roasting tin and add the shallots. Cook, stirring occasionally, until they begin to turn golden.

3 Add the potatoes, parsnips, carrots and remaining garlic cloves. Stir to coat the vegetables in the oil. Season. Place the lamb on top and pour over half the red wine. Cover tightly, place in the oven and cook for 1 hour. Baste occasionally with any fat and juices.

4 Mix together the honey and soy sauce until combined. After the first hour of cooking, pour the honey mixture over the lamb and baste. Return to the oven, uncovered, for a further 1–1¼ hours, basting the meat and vegetables from time to time.

5 Test that the meat is cooked and the vegetables are tender. Remove from the pan and leave the meat to rest for 10–15 minutes before carving (keep the vegetables warm).

6 Place the casserole or roasting tin on the hob, stir in the flour and cook for 1 minute. Blend in the stock and remaining wine, then bring to the boil and adjust the seasoning. Serve the meat and vegetables with plenty of the sauce spooned over them, garnished with fresh rosemary sprigs.

Roast Beef with Yorkshire Puddings

The all-time classic Sunday lunchtime meal reminds us why it's worth keeping this tasty tradition alive.

Serves 6

INGREDIENTS
1.75 kg/4 lb joint of beef, boned and rolled
30–60 ml/2–4 tbsp sunflower oil
300 ml/½ pint/1¼ cups beef stock, wine or water
salt and freshly ground black pepper

FOR THE YORKSHIRE PUDDINGS
50 g/2 oz/½ cup plain flour
1 egg, beaten
150 ml/¼ pint/⅔ cup mixed water and milk
sunflower oil, for cooking

1 Weigh the beef and calculate the cooking time, allowing 15 minutes per 450 g/1 lb plus 15 minutes for rare meat, 20 minutes plus 20 minutes for medium and 25–30 minutes plus 25 minutes for well-done.

2 Preheat the oven to 220°C/425°F/Gas 7. Heat the sunflower oil in a roasting tin in the oven.

3 Place the beef on a rack, fat side on the top, then place the rack in the roasting tin. Baste the beef with the oil, and cook as required, basting occasionally.

6 Spoon off the fat from the roasting tin. Add the stock, wine or water, stirring to dislodge the sediment, and boil for a few minutes. Check the seasoning, then serve with the beef and the Yorkshire puddings.

sunflower oil

joint of beef

plain flour

beef stock

egg

4 To make the Yorkshire puddings, stir the flour and salt and pepper together in a bowl and form a well in the centre. Pour the egg into the well, then slowly pour in the water and milk, stirring in the flour to give a smooth batter. Leave to stand for 30 minutes.

5 A few minutes before the meat is ready, pour a little oil into each of twelve patty tins and place in the oven until very hot. Remove the meat from the oven, season, then cover loosely with foil and keep warm. Quickly divide the batter among the patty tins, then bake for 15–20 minutes, until well risen and golden brown.

COOK'S TIPS
For this roast, choose a boned and rolled joint of sirloin, rib or topside.

To achieve light and crisp Yorkshire puddings, make sure that the patty tins of oil are very hot before adding the batter, then return the tin to the oven immediately – don't allow it to cool. Cook them at the top of the oven for the best results.

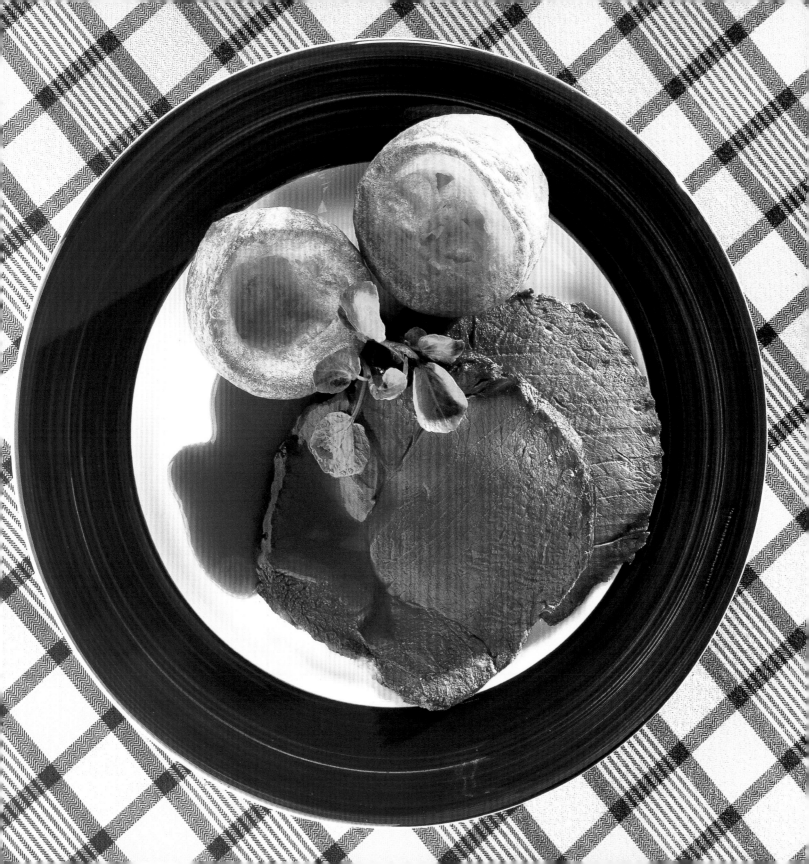

Sausage and Red Onion Pizza

You could substitute fresh Italian spicy sausages in this recipe – they are available from good Italian delicatessens.

Serves 3–4

INGREDIENTS
225 g/8 oz good quality
    pork sausages
5 ml/1 tsp mild chilli powder
2.5 ml/½ tsp freshly ground
    black pepper
30 ml/2 tbsp olive oil
2–3 garlic cloves
1 ready-made pizza base, about
    25–30 cm/10–12 in in diameter
150 ml/¼ pint/⅔ cup tomato sauce
1 red onion, thinly sliced
15 ml/1 tbsp chopped
    fresh oregano
15 ml/1 tbsp chopped fresh thyme
50 g/2 oz mozzarella cheese, grated
50 g/2 oz Parmesan cheese,
    freshly grated

oregano
and thyme   tomato sauce

mozzarella
cheese

red onion   Parmesan
cheese

    olive oil

pork
sausages   garlic   chilli
powder

1 Preheat the oven to 220°C/425°F/ Gas 7. Skin the sausages by running a sharp knife down the side of the skins. Place the sausagemeat in a bowl and add the chilli powder and black pepper; mix well. Break the sausagemeat into walnut-size balls.

2 Heat 15 ml/1 tbsp of the oil in a frying pan and fry the sausage balls for 2–3 minutes until evenly browned.

3 Using a slotted spoon, remove the sausage balls from the pan and drain on kitchen paper.

4 Cut the garlic cloves into thin slices using a small sharp knife.

5 Brush the pizza base with the remaining oil, then spread over the tomato sauce. Scatter over the sausages, garlic, onion and herbs.

6 Sprinkle over the mozzarella and Parmesan and bake for 15–20 minutes until crisp and golden. Serve immediately.

Pepperoni Pizza

This popular pizza, spiced with green chillies and pepperoni, is also known as "American Hot".

Serves 2–3

INGREDIENTS

1 ready-made pizza base, about 25–30 cm/10–12 in in diameter
15 ml/1 tbsp olive oil
115 g/4 oz can peeled and chopped green chillies in brine, drained
150 ml/¼ pint/⅔ cup tomato sauce
75 g/3 oz/¾ cup sliced pepperoni
6 pitted black olives
15 ml/1 tbsp chopped fresh oregano
115 g/4 oz mozzarella cheese, grated
oregano leaves, to garnish

mozzarella cheese

oregano   *tomato sauce*

pepperoni

olive oil

chopped green chillies   *black olives*

1 Preheat the oven to 220°C/425°F/Gas 7. Place the pizza base on a baking sheet and brush evenly all over the top with the oil.

2 Stir the chopped chillies into the tomato sauce, then spread the sauce over the pizza base leaving about 2.5 cm/1 in around the edge clear.

3 Scatter the sliced pepperoni over the sauce.

4 Halve the olives lengthways and scatter them over the sauce with the fresh oregano.

5 Sprinkle the grated mozzarella over the top and bake for 15–20 minutes until the pizza is crisp and golden.

6 Garnish the pizza with oregano leaves and serve immediately.

VARIATION

You can make this pizza as hot as you like. For a really fiery version, use fresh red or green chillies, cut into thin slices, in place of the chillies in brine.

Spaghetti Carbonara

It is said that this dish was originally cooked by Italian coal miners – or charcoal burners – hence the name "carbonara".

Serves 4

INGREDIENTS
175 g/6 oz unsmoked streaky bacon
1 garlic clove, chopped
3 eggs
450 g/1 lb spaghetti
60 ml/4 tbsp freshly grated
   Parmesan cheese
salt and freshly ground black pepper
fresh parsley sprigs, to garnish

eggs

Parmesan cheese

spaghetti

garlic

streaky bacon

parsley

1 Cut the bacon into dice and place in a saucepan. Place over the heat and fry in its own fat with the garlic until brown. Keep warm until needed.

2 Put the eggs in a bowl and whisk together lightly.

3 Cook the spaghetti in a large saucepan of boiling salted water for about 10–12 minutes, or according to the packet instructions until *al dente*. Drain well.

4 Quickly turn the spaghetti into the pan with the bacon and stir in the eggs, a little salt, lots of pepper and half the cheese. Toss well to mix. The eggs should just half cook with the heat from the spaghetti. Serve with the remaining cheese and garnish with fresh parsley.

COOK'S TIP
Be careful not to overcook the egg if you want to achieve a creamy sauce.

Tagliatelle with Bolognese Sauce

Tagliatelle is the traditional pasta for Bolognese sauce, the famous *ragù* from Bologna.

Serves 4

INGREDIENTS
350 g/12 oz dried tagliatelle
shredded fresh basil, to garnish
grated Parmesan cheese, to serve

FOR THE BOLOGNESE SAUCE
30 ml/2 tbsp olive oil
1 onion, finely chopped
1 carrot, finely chopped
1 celery stick, finely chopped
1 garlic clove, crushed
350 g/12 oz/2½ cups minced beef
150 ml/¼ pint/⅔ cup red wine
250 ml/8 fl oz/1 cup milk
400 g/14 oz can chopped tomatoes
15 ml/1 tbsp sun-dried tomato paste
salt and freshly ground black pepper

basil · garlic · onion · carrot · olive oil · minced beef · red wine · tomato paste · chopped tomatoes · milk · celery

COOK'S TIP
Don't skimp on the cooking time – it is essential for a full-flavoured Bolognese sauce. Some Italian cooks insist on cooking it for 3 – 4 hours, so the longer the better.

1 To make the Bolognese sauce, heat the oil in a large saucepan. Add the onion, carrot, celery and garlic and cook gently, stirring frequently, for about 10 minutes until softened. Do not allow the vegetables to colour.

2 Add the minced beef to the pan with the vegetables and cook over a medium heat until the meat changes colour, stirring constantly and breaking up any lumps with a wooden spoon.

3 Pour in the wine. Stir frequently until it has evaporated, then add the milk and continue cooking and stirring until this has evaporated, too.

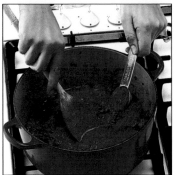

4 Stir in the tomatoes, tomato paste and salt and pepper. Simmer gently, uncovered, for 45 minutes. Cook the tagliatelle in boiling salted water for 8–10 minutes or until *al dente*. Drain, add the sauce and toss to combine. Garnish with basil and serve with Parmesan.

Baked Lasagne

This lasagne, made from egg pasta with home-made Bolognese and béchamel sauces, is truly exquisite.

Serves 8–10

INGREDIENTS
1 recipe Bolognese sauce (see page 83)
400 g/14 oz fresh or dried lasagne
115 g/4 oz/1 cup grated Parmesan cheese
40 g/1½ oz/3 tbsp butter

FOR THE BÉCHAMEL SAUCE
750 ml/1¼ pints/3 cups milk
1–2 bay leaves
3 blades mace
115 g/4 oz/½ cup butter
75 g/3 oz/¾ cup plain flour
salt and freshly ground black pepper

Bolognese sauce *butter* *milk* *bay leaves* *plain flour* *Parmesan cheese* *lasagne*

VARIATION

If you are using dried bought pasta, follow step 5, but boil the lasagne in just two batches, and stop the cooking 4 minutes before the recommended cooking time on the packet has elapsed. Rinse in cold water and lay the pasta out the same way as for egg pasta.

1 Prepare the Bolognese sauce, then set aside. Butter a large shallow baking dish, preferably rectangular or square.

2 Make the béchamel sauce by gently heating the milk with the bay leaves and mace in a small saucepan. Melt the butter in a saucepan. Add the flour, and mix it in well with a wire whisk. Cook for 2–3 minutes.

3 Strain the hot milk into the flour and butter, and mix smoothly with the whisk. Bring the sauce to the boil, stirring constantly, and cook for 4–5 minutes more. Season with salt and pepper, and set aside.

4 If using home-made fresh pasta, cut it into rectangles about 11 cm/4½ in wide and the same length as the baking dish (this will make it easier to assemble). Preheat the oven to 200°C/400°F/Gas 6.

5 Bring a large pan of salted water to the boil. Place a bowl of cold water near the hob. Drop in several of the pasta rectangles and cook briefly, for about 30 seconds. Remove the pasta from the pan and drop into the bowl of cold water for about 30 seconds. Pull them out, shaking off the excess water. Lay them on a dish towel. Continue with the rest of the pasta.

6 To assemble the lasagne, have all the elements at hand: the baking dish, béchamel and meat sauces, pasta strips, grated Parmesan cheese and butter. Spread one large spoonful of the meat sauce over the bottom of the dish. Add a thin layer of béchamel sauce, then arrange a layer of pasta in the dish, cutting it with a sharp knife so that it fits neatly inside the dish.

7 Cover with a thin layer of meat sauce, then one of béchamel. Sprinkle with a little cheese. Repeat the layers in the same order, ending with a layer of pasta coated with béchamel. Sprinkle the top with Parmesan, and dot with butter. Bake for 20 minutes or until brown on top. Remove from the oven and allow to stand for 5 minutes before serving. Serve directly from the baking dish.

Cannelloni with Chicken and Mushrooms

Using chicken makes a lighter alternative to the usual beef-filled, béchamel coated version.

Serves 4–6

INGREDIENTS
450 g/1 lb/4 cups skinless, boneless
  chicken breasts, cooked
225 g/8 oz/2 cups mushrooms
2 garlic cloves, crushed
30 ml/2 tbsp chopped fresh parsley
15 ml/1 tbsp chopped fresh tarragon
1 egg, beaten
fresh lemon juice
12–18 cannelloni tubes
300 ml/½ pint/1¼ cups
  tomato sauce
50 g/2 oz/½ cup freshly grated
  Parmesan cheese
salt and freshly ground black pepper
sprig of fresh parsley, to garnish

egg   *garlic*
  chicken breasts
mushrooms
  lemon
cannelloni
  tomato sauce
parsley
  Parmesan cheese
tarragon

1 Preheat the oven to 200°C/400°F/ Gas 6. Place the chicken in a food processor or blender and process until finely minced. Transfer to a bowl.

2 Place the mushrooms, garlic, parsley and tarragon in the food processor or blender and process until finely minced.

3 Beat the mushroom mixture into the chicken with the egg, salt and pepper and lemon juice to taste.

4 If necessary, cook the cannelloni in plenty of salted boiling water according to the manufacturer's instructions. Drain well on a clean dish towel.

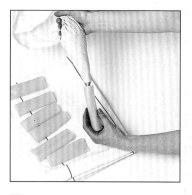

5 Place the filling in a piping bag fitted with a large plain nozzle. Use this to fill each tube of cannelloni.

6 Lay the filled cannelloni tightly together in a single layer in a buttered shallow ovenproof dish. Spoon over the tomato sauce and sprinkle with Parmesan cheese. Bake in the oven for 30 minutes or until brown and bubbling. Serve garnished with a sprig of parsley.

Pastitsio

This simple Greek dish combines pasta, lamb and yogurt in a delicious bake.

Serves 4

INGREDIENTS
15 ml/1 tbsp olive oil
450 g/1 lb/4 cups minced lamb
1 onion, chopped
2 garlic cloves, crushed
30 ml/2 tbsp tomato purée
25 g/1 oz/2 tbsp plain flour
300 ml/½ pint/1¼ cups lamb stock
2 large tomatoes
115 g/4 oz/1 cup pasta shapes
450 g/1 lb tub Greek yogurt
2 eggs
salt and freshly ground black pepper
mixed salad and crusty bread,
    to serve

olive oil   *minced lamb*

garlic   *onion*

tomato purée

Greek yogurt   *plain flour*

tomatoes   *eggs*

lamb stock

pasta shapes

1 Heat the oil in a large pan and fry the lamb for 5 minutes. Add the onion and garlic and continue to fry for a further 5 minutes.

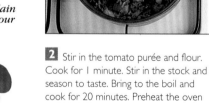

2 Stir in the tomato purée and flour. Cook for 1 minute. Stir in the stock and season to taste. Bring to the boil and cook for 20 minutes. Preheat the oven to 190°C/375°F/ Gas 5.

3 Slice the tomatoes, place the meat in an ovenproof dish and arrange the tomatoes on top.

4 Cook the pasta in plenty of rapidly boiling salted water for 8–10 minutes, or until al dente. Drain thoroughly and mix with the yogurt and eggs. Spoon the pasta mixture on top of the tomatoes and bake for about 1 hour until golden brown and bubbling. Serve hot with a mixed salad and some crusty bread.

VARIATION
Use minced beef in place of the lamb, if you prefer.

Shepherd's Pie

This warming supper dish is an all time favourite, and especially with children.

Serves 4

INGREDIENTS
30 ml/2 tbsp sunflower oil
1 onion, finely chopped
1 carrot, finely chopped
115 g/4 oz mushrooms, chopped
500 g/1¼ lb lean minced lamb
300 ml/½ pint/1¼ cups lamb stock
    or water
15 ml/1 tbsp plain flour
1–2 bay leaves
10–15 ml/2–3 tsp Worcestershire
    sauce
15 ml/1 tbsp tomato purée
675 g/1½ lb potatoes, boiled
25 g/1 oz/2 tbsp butter
45 ml/3 tbsp hot milk
15 ml/1 tbsp chopped
    fresh tarragon
salt and freshly ground black pepper
fresh tarragon sprig, to garnish

milk
mushrooms
carrot
onion
tomato purée
butter
plain flour
Worcestershire sauce
minced lamb
lamb stock
sunflower oil
bay leaves
potatoes
tarragon

1 Heat the oil in a pan, add the onion, carrot and mushrooms and cook, stirring occasionally, until browned. Add the lamb and cook, stirring to break up the lumps, until lightly browned.

2 Blend a few spoonfuls of the stock or water with the flour, then stir this mixture into the pan. Stir in the remaining stock or water and bring to a simmer, stirring. Add the bay leaves, Worcestershire sauce and tomato purée, then cover and cook gently for 1 hour, stirring occasionally. Uncover the pan towards the end of cooking to allow any excess water to evaporate, if needed.

3 Preheat the oven to 190°C/375°F/ Gas 5. Gently heat the potatoes for a couple of minutes, then mash with the butter, milk and seasoning. Add the tarragon and seasoning to the mince and remove and discard the bay leaves, then pour the mince into a pie dish.

4 Cover the mince with an even layer of potato and mark the top with the prongs of a fork. Bake for about 25 minutes, until golden brown. Serve garnished with a fresh sprig of tarragon.

Chicken, Leek and Parsley Pie

A creamy, herby chicken bake encased in crispy puff pastry makes a delicious family meal.

Serves 4–6

INGREDIENTS
FOR THE PASTRY
275 g/10 oz/2½ cups plain flour
pinch of salt
200 g/7 oz/⅞ cup butter, diced
2 egg yolks

FOR THE FILLING
3 part-boned chicken breasts
flavouring ingredients (bouquet
    garni, black peppercorns, onion
    and carrot)
50 g/2 oz/4 tbsp butter
2 leeks, thinly sliced
50 g/2 oz Cheddar cheese, grated
25 g/1 oz Parmesan cheese,
    finely grated
45 ml/3 tbsp chopped fresh parsley
30 ml/2 tbsp wholegrain mustard
5 ml/1 tsp cornflour
300 ml/½ pint/1¼ cups
    double cream
beaten egg, to glaze
salt and freshly ground black pepper
mixed green salad, to serve

Cheddar cheese

butter

leeks

chicken breasts

Parmesan cheese

plain flour

parsley

cornflour

wholegrain mustard

double cream

eggs

1 To make the pastry, first sift the flour and salt. Process the butter and egg yolks in a food processor or blender until creamy. Add the flour and process until the mixture is just coming together. Add about 15 ml/1 tbsp cold water and process for a few seconds more. Turn out on to a lightly floured surface and knead lightly. Wrap in clear film and chill for about 1 hour.

2 Meanwhile, poach the chicken breasts in water to cover, with the flavouring ingredients added, until tender. Leave to cool in the liquid.

3 Preheat the oven to 200°C/400°F/ Gas 6. Divide the pastry into two pieces, one slightly larger than the other. Roll out the large piece and use to line an 18 x 28 cm/7 x 11 in baking dish or tin. Prick the base with a fork and bake for 15 minutes. Leave to cool.

4 Lift the cooled chicken from the poaching liquid and discard the skins and bones. Cut the chicken flesh into strips, then set aside. Melt the butter in a frying pan and fry the leeks over a low heat, stirring occasionally, until soft.

5 Stir in the Cheddar and Parmesan cheeses and chopped parsley. Spread half the leek mixture over the cooked pastry base, leaving a border all the way round. Cover the leek mixture with the chicken strips, then top with the remaining leek mixture.

COOK'S TIP

This pastry is quite fragile and may break; the high fat content, however, means that you can patch it together by pressing pieces of pastry trimmings into any cracks that may appear.

6 Mix together the mustard, cornflour and cream in a small bowl. Add salt and pepper to taste. Pour over the filling.

7 Moisten the edges of the cooked pastry base. Roll out the remaining pastry and use to cover the pie. Brush with beaten egg and bake for 30–40 minutes until golden and crisp. Serve hot, cut into square portions, with a green salad.

Chicken and Ham Pie

This domed double-crust pie is excellent for a cold buffet, for picnics or any packed meals.

Serves 8

INGREDIENTS

400 g/14 oz shortcrust pastry
800 g/1¾ lb chicken breasts
350 g/12 oz uncooked gammon
about 60 ml/4 tbsp double cream
6 spring onions, finely chopped
15 ml/1 tbsp chopped
    fresh tarragon
10 ml/2 tsp chopped fresh thyme
grated rind and juice of
    ½ large lemon
5 ml/1 tsp freshly ground mace
beaten egg or milk, to glaze
salt and freshly ground black pepper

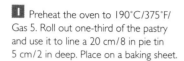

shortcrust pastry

chicken breasts

gammon

spring onions

double cream

tarragon

thyme

lemon

1 Preheat the oven to 190°C/375°F/Gas 5. Roll out one-third of the pastry and use it to line a 20 cm/8 in pie tin 5 cm/2 in deep. Place on a baking sheet.

2 Mince 115 g/4 oz of the chicken with the gammon, then mix with the cream, spring onions, herbs, lemon rind, 15 ml/1 tbsp of the lemon juice and the seasoning to make a soft mixture; add more cream if necessary.

3 Cut the remaining chicken into 1 cm/½ in pieces and mix with the remaining lemon juice, the mace and salt and pepper.

COOK'S TIP

Make sure, when you are rolling out the pastry and lining the pie tin, that you don't stretch the pastry, otherwise it will shrink during cooking.

4 Make a layer of one-third of the gammon mixture in the pastry base, cover with half the chopped chicken, then add another layer of one-third of the gammon. Add all the remaining chicken followed by the remaining gammon mixture. Dampen the edges of the pastry base. Roll out the remaining pastry to make a lid for the pie.

5 Use the trimmings to make a lattice decoration. Make a small hole in the centre of the pie, brush the top with beaten egg or milk, then bake for about 20 minutes. Reduce the temperature to 160°C/325°F/Gas 3 and bake for a further 1–1¼ hours; cover the top with foil if the pastry becomes too brown. Transfer the pie to a wire rack and leave to cool.

Quiche Lorraine

The classic quiche, a delicious mixture of crumbly crust, custardy filling and smoky bacon flavour.

Serves 6

INGREDIENTS
350 g/12 oz shortcrust pastry
225 g/8 oz smoked streaky bacon
    rashers, chopped
3 eggs
2 egg yolks
350 ml/12 fl oz/1½ cups
    whipping cream
120 ml/4 fl oz/½ cup milk
salt and freshly ground black pepper

shortcrust pastry

streaky bacon

eggs

milk

whipping cream

VARIATIONS
Replace the bacon with diced cooked ham, and add 75 g/3 oz grated Gruyère cheese.

For a vegetarian quiche, omit the bacon. Slice 450 g/1 lb courgettes and fry in a little oil until lightly browned on both sides. Drain on kitchen paper, then arrange in the flan case. Scatter 50 g/2 oz grated cheese on top. Make the egg mixture with 4 eggs, 250 ml/8 fl oz/1 cup cream, 60 ml/4 tbsp milk, ⅛ tsp grated nutmeg, and salt and pepper.

1 Preheat the oven to 200°C/400°F/ Gas 6. Roll out the pastry thinly and use to line a 23 cm/9 in flan tin. Prick the pastry base with a fork, then line with greaseproof paper and fill with baking beans. Bake "blind" for 15 minutes, then remove the paper and beans.

2 Fry the bacon in a frying pan until it is crisp and golden brown. Drain the bacon on kitchen paper.

3 Scatter the bacon in the partially baked flan case.

4 In a bowl, whisk together the eggs, egg yolks, cream and milk. Season with salt and pepper. Pour the egg mixture into the flan case.

5 Bake the quiche for 35–40 minutes or until the filling is set and golden brown and the pastry is golden. Serve warm or at room temperature.

Guinness and Beef Pie with Oysters

Layers of crisp puff pastry encase a tasty rich stew of tender beef and fresh oysters.

Serves 4

INGREDIENTS
450 g/1 lb stewing beef
30 ml/2 tbsp plain flour
15 ml/1 tbsp sunflower oil
30 ml/2 tbsp butter
1 onion, sliced
150 ml/¼ pint/⅔ cup Guinness
150 ml/¼ pint/⅔ cup beef stock
5 ml/1 tsp sugar
1 bouquet garni
12 oysters, opened
350 g/12 oz puff pastry
1 egg, beaten
salt and freshly ground black pepper
chopped fresh parsley, to garnish

stewing beef

plain flour

egg

beef stock

onion

Guinness

puff pastry   *butter*   *sunflower oil*

bouquet garni   *oysters*

1 Preheat the oven to 180°C/350°F/Gas 4. Trim any excess fat from the meat and cut into 2.5 cm/1 in pieces. Place the meat in a bag with the flour and plenty of seasoning. Shake until all the meat is well coated.

3 Pour the Guinness and stock into the casserole, then add the sugar and bouquet garni. Cover and cook in the oven for 1¼ hours.

4 Remove the casserole from the oven and discard the bouquet garni. Spoon the beef and Guinness mixture into a large pie dish and set aside to cool for about 15 minutes. Increase the oven temperature to 200°C/400°F/Gas 6.

COOK'S TIP
The oysters are a delicious addition to this traditional Irish pie, but they are not essential. Omit them, if you prefer.

2 Heat the oil and butter in a flameproof casserole and fry the meat for 10 minutes until well sealed and browned all over. Add the sliced onion and continue cooking for 2–3 minutes until just softened.

5 Meanwhile, remove the oysters from their shells and wash. Dry on kitchen paper and stir into the beef and Guinness mixture.

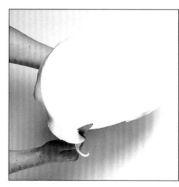

6 Roll out the pastry to fit the pie dish. Brush the edge of the dish with the beaten egg and lay the pastry over the top. Trim neatly and decorate. Brush with the remaining egg and bake for 25 minutes until puffed and golden. Serve immediately garnished with parsley.

INDEX